Don't Get Boned

The Harm City Handbook

Dust Cover
This urban survival guide answers dozens of self-defense and avoidance questions, including:
What can I legally defend myself with while in public spaces?

How should I defend my home and family?

How do I wear my back pack to minimizing muggings?

What are the dangers of using a car in the urban environment?

What are the keys to avoidance and the clues to predicting assailant behavior?

Don't Get Boned is a handbook for surviving the nuanced threats of postmodern urban life, written for the person residing in the hunting matrix outside of law enforcement.

Books by James LaFond

Nonfiction
The Fighting Edge, 2000
The Logic of Steel, 2001
The First Boxers, 2011
The Gods of Boxing, 2011
All Power Fighting, 2011
When You're Food, 2011
The Lesser Angles of Our Nature, 2012
The Logic of Force, 2012
The Greatest Boxer, 2012
Take Me to Your Breeder, 2014
The Streets Have Eyes, 2014
Panhandler Nation, 2014
The Ghetto Grocer, 2014
American Fist, 2014
Don't Get Boned, 2014
Alienation Nation, 2014
In The Chinks of The Machine, 2014
How the Ghetto Got My Soul, 2014
Saving the World Sucks, 2014
Taboo You, 2014
The Fighting Life, 2014
Narco Night Train, 2014
Into the Mountains of Madness, 2014

Fiction
Astride the Chariot of Night, 2014
Sacrifix, 2014
Rise, 2014

Motherworld, 2014
Planet Buzzkill, 2014
Fruit of The Deciever, 2014
Forty Hands of Night, 2014
Black and Pale, 2014
Daughters of Moros, 2014
Fat Girl, 2014
Hurt Stoker, 2014
Poet, 2014
Triumph, 2015
Winter, 2015
The Spiral Case, 2015
Hemavore, with Dominick Mattero, 2015
Yusuf of the Dusk, 2015
Mantid, 2015
RetroGenesis: Day 1, with Erique Watson, 2015

Sunset Saga Novels
Big Water Blood Song, 2011
Ghosts of the Sunset World, 2011
Beyond the Ember Star, 2012
Comes the Six Winter Night, 2012
Thunder-Boy, 2012
The World is Our Widow, 2013
Behind the Sunset Veil, 2013
Den of The Ender, 2013
God's Picture Maker, 2014
Out of Time, 2015
Seven Moons Deep, 2015

Don't Get Boned

For Quinn a man with a racket

Contents

Preface

I have been writing magazine articles and books on how not to get boned since 1996. It is really an endless subject bordered by many conditional and malleable societal factors. Not getting boned is quite frankly an endlessly evolving art that we have been practicing since the beginning, whether that beginning was shoving a tapir bone up a leopard's ass or kicking that apple eating bitch out of the best crib a dude ever had.

Surviving is the way of men, and in my experience, it is best and most often accomplished with what is between your ears, not what is between your hands, though what is hanging between your legs is to a certain extent a requisite. Character—a calm considered kind of social courage—is the prime requisite for making the advice given in these pages work. If you are a person who reads—even if a coward—you are halfway there. Brawn is not the way, not for long, not in a predatory environment. The baddest dudes I have known have been put into the ground or into a wheel chair at the end of a lesser man's gun.

Please, as you consider the advice herein realize that it is not total or absolute and that its purpose is developing the art of avoidance.

James, Sunday, 10/19/14

The Aggression Matrix

A Comprehensive Scale for Defining Violence / Or, A Public Service For Those Who Do Not Wish To Become Criminal Food

© 2011 James LaFond

Disclaimer: I have tried to put my unacceptable opinions in brackets. But they're virulent you know.

Preface

As "The Violence Guy" I have often been questioned by people curious about defining their own experiences. I have also interviewed many people who only thought of their violent experiences in a single context, discounting the rest as something 'other'. A crime victim may define that act as violence or not. If they define it as violence then childhood fights they experienced may not—in their mind—be regarded as violent acts.

There is also the question often put to me about my surviving crime, considering my impoverished urban lifestyle. Being a pedestrian does bring additional exposure in urban environs. A pedestrian is more easily spotted, the predators have more time to consider how his demise can benefit them with the least risk, and there are a lot less of us pedestrians on the menu than you zooming motorists, inconsiderately bypassing the ambushes so thoughtfully arranged by your local hardworking criminal.

Let us just say it's is all about recognizing a developing situation and making sure that you keep it from escalating. This will become self-evident once you examine the matrix below. This is the tool I use to regulate my behavior in the face of aggression. The personal results have not been a great feeding of the ego. But, I have remained a thankfully obscure item on the local criminal menu; that not-so-fresh blowfish prepared by the novice sushi chef with the shaking hand...

Concept

Let me begin to clear the air by equating violence and aggression. It is best to conceive of these two terms as alternate descriptions of 'coercion backed by threat of force and/or the application of force to injure, maim, violate or kill'. Because the term *violence* is more often equated with vigorous physical effort and resulting injury I have generally abandoned it in favor of the term *aggression*, which has broader connotations. There is a very real semantic dilemma here. Engaging in aggression—even verbally—is to step onto a very slippery slope. The most common misunderstanding harbored by the subjects of my study and people who I discuss the study with, is that most define an act as violence or aggression only if it is marked by confrontation and the physical use of force, generally discounting threats, even lethal ones.

Examples:

1. A security guard who apprehends a shoplifter through verbal or 'light touch' compliance will not mark this as an act of aggression or violence, although the shoplifter and her spouse will hold quite a different view.
2. The mother of a jilted woman who threatens to "kill" the former boyfriend does not believe herself to be engaged in violence, but the fleeing Don Juan might disagree.

3. The police officer who placed his hand on his holstered weapon as he approached me on a darkened street at 11:08 PM Wednesday December 7th 2011, was, in his mind, acting defensively. I saw it in another light, as a state-sponsored act of aggression that violated my supposed freedom to walk to work unmolested by body-armored wearers of Bat Man utility belts. [Isn't that in the *Bill of Rights* somewhere? Oh, that's right they didn't have Bat Man back then.]

4. A man who threatened people with heavy tools in collecting debts for a drug dealer as an adult did not consider that his fist fights with neighborhood boys in his childhood rated as acts of aggression or violence.

5. A prize-fighter robbed at gunpoint described the act as a property crime rather than an act of violence or aggression. The ATM had robbed him just seconds earlier!

6. When I barred the entrance to a criminal when acting as a doorman by extending my open hand to come just short of his face I recognized that that non-contact act was indeed the initiation of hostilities. Since he outweighed me by 260 pounds I palmed an ink pen with my hidden hand so I could push

it into some soft part if he decided to trample me. Neither of us chose to escalate, with him backing down. [If I were a practitioner of some esoteric Asian art I might claim to have submitted him with my "chi". But I am not a chi master, just a humble American sorcerer who summoned an elder demon out of the nighted abyss to shatter this barbarian's fragile resolve!]

I use the list below to put acts of aggression in context. Consider cataloguing your own life experiences by assigning each a number from this table. Also consider each number to represent a wide-range of behavior that might like-wise constitute an escalating matrix. I have survived dozens of violent crimes by managing them in the '0' to '4' zone. People ask "How can you know?" Those people don't have a clue and just need to stay locked down in their zooming vehicles. [Really, if it breaks down, call out of work. Don't take the bus, you're already dead.]

The Aggression Matrix
0. Threat, verbal
1. Threat, by posturing [body-language]
2. Threat, by brandishing [presenting a weapon]
3. Threat, by touching [a narrow but common

predicament]

4. Threat, by a push, hold, lock or by touching/measuring with weapon
5. Mutual Combat, or "fight" between willing [idiots] individuals
6. Battery, aggression by unarmed strike
7. Injury
8. Disability or maiming
9. Violation, torture and mutilation
10. Killing
11. Over-killing, postmortem atrocities & other TV crime-drama nastiness

Threat Nuances

Please carefully consider the threat end of the scale. Manipulation of this range of aggression is what keeps you off of the top of the scale. It is the duty* of every civilized person [Yes, blame me for the 'barbarism' defense, please.] to maintain an encounter and manage it in the *threat zone*.

A careful consideration of '0' and '1' should reveal to any rational person [Yes, both of you.] a veritable escalation scale for each. Consider the difference in body language from cowering in a fetal position, to shrinking back with hands in pockets, to putting out the conciliatory hand, to warning off an approaching person with the staying hand, to hovering with grinding teeth and clenching hands, to snarling at their soft throat with your slathering snout...

"I'm good. Thanks—the happy pill—the pink one in my shirt pocket. Deep breath..."

Think of the verbal range alone. You can hop on the scale with anything from "I don't want any trouble sir" [even if he is only thirteen-years-old] to "I'm going to eat your children!" [He's thirteen-years-old isn't he—a baby's daddy by now.]

*I know that sounded preachy—grated in my mind in fact. But it is still called 'civilization' you know. Just thought it was worth a heads up.

Mutual Combat

This is its own *stupidity zone*, and is easily a point of departure into the threat zone where many mutual combats end up being terminated as things deescalate due to exhaustion or the appearance of Mom—or for adults, the police. In court this comes down to 'no harm, no foul' [so long as nobody

pissed off the cop or called the judge a dyke] or
made the *order-of-magnitude miscalculation!*

Getting Cozy with the Order-of-Magnitude Miscalculation

Getting into battery can result in a slide all the way
up the scale until someone is having their brains
kicked out against a curb. I did not structure this
end of the scale based on intent. Determining the
intention of the combatant you did not get to
interview is very difficult for the third-person
researcher. This is all about results, and based on
the possibilities implicate in the table above, Hell is
the limit. I really want to call this the boned zone.
Oh, I just did. Charles, should I bracket that? The
use of weapons to do harm takes you right to seven
as a starting point. Legally, this is where battery
escalates into larger legal liabilities.

Weapons will take you very quickly to 10.
According to our bankrupt society's malleable
mores the actions listed as Level Nine are more
heinous or equal to killing. Being a practical person
I rate killing as worse—even though it often takes
less effort—because the dead can't fight back,
unless, of course, their powers of chi may still be

accessed in the hereafter and projected back into the world of the living. I have yet to meet a kung fu master that makes that claim. But I'm sure he is out there.

Be safe, say no to the *boned zone* and keep it in the *threat zone*.

James, December 11th 2011

Managing Violence

Guidelines for Dealing with Convergence Predation

© 2012 James LaFond

The following information is derived from the author's own experiences working as a retail food manager from 2006 thru 2010, and working security for a collectable card tournament organizer from 2009 thru 2011.

Caution

I can offer criminal profiles, and tips for managing violence. But I am not a self-defense instructor. In the vast majority of cases you can successfully deal with a criminal from a position of authority [even if that position is just a shift-manager position at a retail store] without things getting physical. However, if you manage a high volume operation long enough, the sheer quantity of hostile human beings that you must deal with will eventually result in a physical altercation. You should have a self-defense instructor if you are in such a position. You or your instructor will have to provide the physical answers to the scenarios that are prone to develop in case you must physically deal with the types of criminals discussed below.

Context

In four years as a retail food manager I logged 2,908 incidents on my calendar, usually with just two letters to indicate an event: PH for panhandler, etc. The criminals I dealt with included from most to least frequent: drunks [usually attempting late access after closing time before a holiday or on the weekend]; panhandlers; shoplifters; gangs of youths; organized thieves; blitz shoplifters; drug-dealers; bootleg DVD vendors; perverts attempting to molest my female staff; terminated employees; strong-arm robbers working the parking lot and approaches [seven of my male clerks were attacked leaving work]; counterfeit bill rings; purse-snatchers; slip & fall con artists; and even two police officers who threatened me for not opening up the store for their personal use after hours.

As a clerk in this business for 25 years, I knew going in that there would be little or no backup from whoever I hired to do security work. Security personnel who work retail [including uniformed and off-duty police] are generally only concerned with one thing: socializing with your female staff. That is my experience working 34 retail outlets in Baltimore City and Baltimore County from 1981 thru 2011. I hate to label a profession but this is my experience and I will argue it with anyone. I'm sure this is not always the case, but this fact was one of the parameters that I was aware of going in. Local law-enforcement has always provided me with adequate backup in each of the three municipalities I worked. However, as effective as this backup might be, it is ten minutes away. I was essentially alone, and developed methods within that parameter.

Of the 2,908 incidents that I was personally involved in only three became physical: I wrestled with a knife-wielding shoplifter, recovering his coat, both of his knives, and all 72 bars of my soap he had stuffed in the lining of his coat; I was struck by a clerk I terminated [Thank you for winning the unemployment case for me sir.]; and I was grappled by, and head-butted a mentally disturbed panhandler. That is it; solid proof that people in positions of authority can manage violence and do not have to get physical often.

This type of situation, when you are stuck in a high volume location that attracts criminals like hyenas to a watering hole, is a type of Convergence Predation. Adopting a siege mentality will result in the erosion of your position, such as it is. You must be proactive in an appropriate sense. That means calming down the young lady and the old drunk who are fighting over their place in the express lane as the blizzard rolls up the East Coast and everyone else in the building is panicking over the End of Time and the sold out slot in the DVD vending machine!

It also means dropping your box cutter and leaping over that display you are building without taking the time to apologize to the customer who is discussing the football game with you so that you can make it to that sore-covered dope fiend on the parking lot that is trying to get to the old lady with the walker while your security guard sleeps at the video monitoring station.

These tips can be generalized to events and permanent businesses, but are intended for the businessman. For tips specific to countering Event

Predation as a dedicated security operative see my soon-to-be Noble nominated book **When You're Food**.

The Keys to Managing Violence

The key to my success was how I used my position. Every person I dealt with—even the two cops, who were out of their municipality—knew that the cops who responded would believe the guy wearing the tie and the name badge. So they opted for the negotiated solution I offered. If you find yourself in such a position, managing violence, either as a security person, or as a manager, here is a quick checklist of does and don'ts:

1. Never raise your voice.
2. Address the criminal with respect [especially if he is a cop], as 'sir', or if a boy, as 'man'
3. Never embarrass the criminal. Try to approach him when he is alone, so that you can avoid putting him under pressure to appear strong in front of others. He wants to be weak. He wants you to be his daddy or his big brother. Befriending criminals that frequent your establishment is good policy. If you help this guy by delivering groceries to

his crippled father while he's in prison, and give him tips on how to speak to the cops—who are, after all, on the way—then you have taken the moral high ground and he will tend do what you ask him to do. He can also be cultivated as an intelligence asset.

4. Do not use confrontational body language. Stand obliquely and do not hide your right hand or place your hands between him and you, and never, ever point. Yes, you are placing yourself in danger. You are there to protect others—even this scumbag—not protect yourself. You will not sue yourself. Every employee, customer and criminal will sue you and your employer if injured on premises. What I actually practiced was self-defense against lawyers, not criminals. The criminal is just going to break your glasses, not your bank account.

5. Never touch anybody unless you really have to prevent a crime. I have even been able to retrieve steaks from shoplifters by only touching their clothes. If you have to touch try clothing first. Do everything you can to avoid hurting the criminal. Remember the deranged guy that I could not handle in the clinch? I head-butted him in the forehead,

intentionally avoiding his nose, which could have exploded. But I was still not pleased with this resolution. The fact that it went physical at all meant that I had failed to manage the situation.

6. To protect someone, like the old lady who is trying to run the gauntlet of screaming, drug-addicted, sore-covered panhandlers so that she can buy the jumbo eggs you put on sale for a dollar, all you have to do is get in the way. You do not have to be big or intimidating or even armed. You just have to escort people to protect them from common criminals. You are a meat shield in slacks and tie; Miss Ann's very own Secret Service Agent, bad haircut and all.

7. Never, ever show anger or use bad language. You must always be calm, cool and polite to derive the maximum benefit from your position, which is one of respect. You are the calm, cooling hand. Stay cool, even when you are burning up inside. This last, is the health hazard of the job. I, for one, could only tolerate four consecutive years as the benign stepfather to a hundred employees [who are prone to various antisocial behaviors] and

the sheepdog to a flock of customers who are hunted by the wolves of society.

What about the Humble Employee?

You are pretty much screwed. Really, when you leave work you're just bloody meat thrown into shark-infested waters. However, I am supposed to offer some comforting advice...

If it is not your job to deal with problem people you can still use the guidelines above to diffuse potentially violent situations. However, you must be more careful and will have less success. Much of the potency of the above techniques is based on the supposition that the local police will back up the manager. If you are just the clerk headed home from work you are a more likely target than the manager, and will not derive the benefit he does from his status. In fact, after the punks mug you they may well have you arrested for assault.

The calm cool demeanor approach that is mandatory for managers can be helpful against street criminals because they may equate your lack of agitation with lack of fear, and your fear is one of their enabling devices. Staying cool will also serve you well after you have effectively defended yourself and the cops lock in on your heat signature. Remember, in the eyes of law enforcement, the criminal is the person who has effectively used force, and the victim is the one on the ground, even if he was a mugger. If you have just effectively defended yourself you will have to convince the suspicious responding officer that you did not unjustly usurp his exclusive right to use force.

Conclusion

Let the cops beat them down. Remember, your ultimate duty is to provide your obese clients with the most efficient delivery systems for sodium, caffeine and simple carbohydrates at affordable prices, in a safe and congenial environment. That's best accomplished with your shirt tucked in.

Anatomy of a Knockout

An Abridged Archive from the Violence Project

© 2012 James LaFond

Yesterday Eric Painter, a member of a military combatives group in Texas, called me about this old article on behalf of a member of his group that is currently on duty in Afghanistan. If a dude getting shot at by the guys that boned the Soviets wants something it gets top priority here. I looked up the old floppy file and found a mess of manually spaced tables that would drive Charles crazy. So I am editing the thing and re-formatting it so it can be posted by the 29th.

Thanks for the heads up Eric.

-James LaFond, 4/24/2012

Author's Note: When my wife handed me the phone and told me it was the FBI just a few weeks after 911 I thought for sure they had found a copy of *The Logic of Steel* in a terrorist's hotel room. As visions of me being water-boarded live on Fox News flashed across my mind and I contemplated if my $364.00 royalty check was really worth ostracism and torture, I got to know the voice of Agent Tom Petrowski. Tom had read my Black Belt material and interviewed me extensively about my own interview and record keeping process. I then interviewed him about an encounter to demonstrate my approach.

Tom was looking for help talking the Department Of Justice nerds out of sending us back to Rodney King Land. Apparently, after some fat crack-head died of heart failure while being choked, the DOJ basically told the FBI [and by extension the other law-enforcement agencies around the country] to go back to beating people until they submit. Tom requested an incapacitation study, and I did my best. I doubt however if it helped him. After the virulent statements I made about law enforcement and the judiciary in my books I don't think anything I publish will be taken seriously by the DOJ.

Look, what follows is just a bunch of percentages.

In the meantime, in all of your self-defense encounters, please strive to remain to the right of this % symbol. Being to the left is not good.

Anatomy of the Knockout: A Comprehensive Study of the Circumstances & Effects of 512 Violent Encounters That Resulted In A Knockout

The following analysis is derived from the author's original study of 1675 acts of violence compiled between June 1996 and May 2000. These 512 acts of violence represent 33% of all violence, and resulted in the incapacitation as a result of impact (not exhaustion or choke) of 534 individuals. The study of these 534 incapacitations has been undertaken at the request of Supervisory Special Agent Tom D. Petrowski of the Legal Instruction Unit, FBI Academy at Quantico VA

The median KO rate is 33%.
Any aspect of violence (i.e. a drunken defender) associated with a KO rate of 34% or better should be regarded as a KO indicator.
All aspects associated with a KO rate of 32% or less should be regarded as KO counter-indicators.

Situations
Inside: 39% of indoor action resulted in a KO
Outside: 29% of outdoor action results in a KO
Night: 32% of nocturnal violence results in a KO
Day: 32% of daytime violence results in a KO.
Attack: 34% of attacks result in a KO.
Fight: 29% of mutual combats result in a KO.

Alcohol: 36% of drunks inflict KOs; 35% of drunks are KO'd

Law enforcement actions: 27% of law-enforcement or Security actions result in a KO

On the job violence: 27% of those attacked on the job are KO'd

Female aggressors: 20% of female aggressors inflict KOs

Female defenders: 21% of female defenders KO'd

Group aggressions: 45% of group aggressors inflict KOs

Group defenders: 61% of group defenders suffer KOs to one or more member of the group

Armed aggressor: 37% of armed aggressors inflict KOs

Armed defender: 45% of armed defenders inflict KOs

Trained aggressor: 39% of trained aggressors inflict KOs

Trained defender: 29% of trained defenders inflict KOs

Grappling: 32% of grappling situations result in a KO

Floor fights: 18% of floor fights result in KO

Duration
1-10 seconds: 25% of short actions result in a KO

10-60 seconds: 35% of mid-length actions result in a KO

Over 60 seconds: 45% of long actions result in

incapacitations, indicating multiple strikes as a primary cause.

Method

Throw: 62% of throws result in KOs*

Punch: 28% of KOs result from punching

Butt/Smash/Stomp: 75% of butting, smashing & stomping acts result in KOs*

*These results indicate that the actual fighting surface accounts for a lot of damage.

Kick/knee: 80% of kickers inflict KOs [I interviewed some sadistic kick-boxers.]

Low-impact note: Holds, slaps, chokes & pushing constitute the dominant activity in 30% of all violence.

Choke note: there were only 3 resolutions via choke in 1675 acts.

Combination method: only 17% of KOs resulted from integrated fighting methods or combined tactics. This generally reflected successful defenses and controlling behavior. This suggests that a skilled and versatile combatant, can by their vary inclusion in the encounter, limit the level of violence.

Results

Aggressor medical: 7%

Defender medical: 24%

Aggressor legal: 23%

Defender legal: 7%

Death: 87% of violent deaths are suffered by defender

Q: How often was someone KO'd by an open hand martial arts blow?

Twice: a heel-palm to the chin and a double palm to the chest. One other such blow was attempted (a knife-hand to the throat) which failed. Although 30% of KO situations involved a trained fighter (law-officer, boxer, wrestler, martial artist, kick-boxer) the attempted use of open hand blows was statistically insignificant. The 33% rate of success with open hand blows compares unfavorably to the 73% incidence of overall success. Only 23% of aggressions are not decisive. Keep in mind that numbers this small tend to provide skewed results.

Q: What are the most effective specific one-strike KO methods?

100% success: Sucker-punches by competition level boxers to the jaw of individual.

100% success: Lateral outward ice-pick stab to face of chest.

98% success: Surprise come-from-behind strikes with heavy blunt weapons to the head of an intoxicated male.

95% success: Poor-leverage throws by males averaging 290 pounds against smaller members of aggressive groups and individual participants in match fights.

90% success: Punches thrown by an average-size athletic man against unprepared members of a poorly organized aggressive group.
90%: 'Sucker-kicks' by trained fighters.

Sports Models

19% of karate stylists who had no kick-boxing experience KO'd their opponents in violent situations. This is identical to the worldwide kick-boxing KO ratio of 19%.

20% of boxers KO'd their antagonist compared to the 34% worldwide boxing KO ratio. These were often urban street encounters that featured groups, weapons & indecisive resolutions.

90% of boxers involved in drunken brawls KO'd their opponents with 10% sustaining hand injuries. Not one of these boxers jabbed.

36% of martial artists with kick-boxing experience KO'd their antagonist. These encounters reflect a wide variety of circumstances and correspond to the worldwide boxing KO ratio. The side-kick was the dominant KO strike.

47% of identified non-combat athletes scored KOs in brawls and self-defense situations. These were primarily large throwers (football players) and small punchers (rugby, softball & soccer players) taking the fight to low-cohesion groups of smaller or softer males.

Knockout Rates by Weapon Type
Firearm: 28%
Edged: 31%
Folding Knife: 19%
Fixed-blade knife: 38%
Pencil: 13%
Pointed tools: 44%
Prison-made shank: 64%
Razor: 5% (2 out of 40)
Sword: 33% (4 out of 12)
Blunt: 39%
Stick/baton: 37% (law officer); 20% (escrimador); 28% (untrained); 27% (group)
Bat: 58%
Board/club: 70%
Pipe/bar: 36%
Sap/black-jack/whip-stick: 47%
Stone/brick/trophy: 56% (individual); 88% (group)
Blunt tools: 42%
Machinery/Furniture: 42%
Everyday items like bottles: 20% (by defender); 7% (by aggressor)

Conclusion

In retrospect, after looking over these percentages, and having used them as a reference for my violence books and articles, I think we should look at the weapon types above and the likely-hood of their use to inflict knockouts less as a forensic question and more as a behavioral one. Look to the weapon, its employment, and its type as indications of intent and resolve. Comparing the prison shank to the sword is a perfect example of how much violence is invested in the mind as opposed to the tool. Look to the tool and the relationship the user forms with it as a reflection of their mindset.

Here is to staying to the right.

Why You Are Food

The Social Mechanics of Alienation

© 2012 James LaFond

Most people, good & bad, black, white, yellow, red and brown—and those little green creeps that trashed Mars and are now skulking around in the Kyber Belt prepared to launch a comet at us when the ancient Mayan astronomers finally give them the okay—believe that victims are selected along racial lines. In traditional and largely homogenous societies this has been the case. For instance, in Medieval Europe the Jews and the Gypsies were routinely targeted for violence because they were aliens living on the fringe of a cohesive society that adhered to certain hates actually perpetuated by the Church and State. Seen in this light the Final Solution simply exposes Hitler as the last and most prolific in a millennia-long string of superstitious purveyors of mass hysterical hatred.

The Land of Predatory Possibility and Home of the Craven

In our current American world we live in a society where the Church [all of them] and State [all of them, and the big federal one too] discourage any type of violence except that committed by the State. This State also sets aside particularly stiff penalties for attacking people belonging to minority racial groups. Just as the blood-thirsty medieval robber/rapist sought to avoid divine retribution by only preying upon those that were seen as enemies of Heaven, the modern predator seeks to attack prey in such a manner as to minimize his chances of being preyed upon by the State. This is best accomplished by hunting alienated members of society. This is mainly to limit the number of witnesses that might be sympathetic to the victim. Other measures are also taken, such as choosing not to use the widely available firearms at our disposal and by making certain to attack as a member of a pack, thus dividing the legal risk.

Of course, one's state of alienation fluctuates from time-to-time and place-to-place, and may sometimes fall into the ancient pattern of racial violence. However, race is not the motive. If twenty Mexicans are gathering to attack someone, anyone, they will of course be on the lookout for a black or white target. But, if this cannot be found they will attack a Salvadoran. If a Salvadoran is not available they will attack another Mexican. You see, in modern America alienation is not the bloody feuding quilt of ethnic antagonisms and alliances that it once was, but is rather a constant fluctuating state of predation. The modern American is not a moral citizen of a city, town or subdivision, but an amoral inhabitant of a hunting matrix, where someone can always be found to occupy the alienation bubble that slides along the societal level.

If you doubt this assertion that our society is one of profound alienation, look at network and cable television. For the past ten years the most successful show has been Survivor [to me the embodiment of evil], which has nothing to do with survival. This show is nothing but a contest in alienating others. Every reality show has successfully followed this model; division, alienation, and exile. The mass of Americans spend more leisure time watching ritualized alienation than in any other pursuit. In my mind this is the apogee of barbarism. When the ancients exiled someone it was to cast them out among the unwashed barbarians. Now, we live in a society where nearly everyone fantasizes about becoming the only person to escape alienation, and in the process win a million dollars, by successfully alienating all of those around us, and hence, ultimately sit in a state of supreme unchallenged alienation and comfort.

What type of society could possibly be more perverse?

If you live in certain cultural enclaves the predation matrix may still resemble the ancient one. In such a case, if you are a black man, you best not walk into that trailer park, and if you are a Mexican you better not try to get a job at that construction site, and if you are a skinny white guy who is the only pale face at Gunpowder State Park you just might want to kick yourself in the butt for showing up with the best looking black chick on your arm...

Now, as bad as the situations outlined in the paragraph above seem, they are easily avoidable—for instance I could have dated her ugly sister instead...

The real and relatively unavoidable threat which requires you to be on constant alert like a U.S. Marine in a war zone, is finding yourself in a predation matrix, where there is always the chance that you will suddenly make it onto the menu.

Are You Food?

Are you on the menu? If so, are you ala carte, or perhaps just desert?

To find out ask yourself the following questions and imagine how most of the people you come into daily contact with would first respond upon hearing of the crime in question. If you answer 'yes' to all of them you are a main dish. If you answer yes to most of them you are ala carte. If those you know would answer yes to some of them, congratulations, you are desert, and provided the entree portion size was large enough your attackers may be satiated before they notice that you come with a nice candy-red glaze...

1. If your ass-kissing coworker leaves his coat in the lunchroom next to the door by the men's room [that is regularly used by homeless men] and then has his coat stolen, is it at least partially his fault that his coat was stolen? Shouldn't he have left it in the office or locked it in his locker?

2. If the ugly twerp across the street gets drunk and then walks to the liquor store and pays for his gin with a twenty peeled off of a knot-roll of bills as thick as your fist, then gets jumped by the three criminals who were standing behind him, wasn't he at least a little responsible for his robbery? I mean, shouldn't he have just taken a $20 with him? Or should he have just stayed home after getting drunk?

3. If the smoking hot chick across the street who your wife hates for some unfathomable reason leaves her house wearing nothing but a bikini and is groped by the wino that sleeps in the gutter in front or your house because your mother-in-law feeds him pickled eggs at 9:15 AM, is it her fault for being a slut? Really, are you going to agree with your wife here too? Or might it be your bat-shit-crazy mother-in-law's fault? If you answer yes to any version of this question you are part of the problem—now stop staring at her while you pretend to be concerned for her dignity...

4. If the old retired guy next-door decides to walk his obnoxious ever-yipping lapdog in the alley behind your house, and gets jumped by the junkies that smoke crack back there is it his fault for insisting it's still the 1950s? Is it the cops' fault for

not policing the alley? Is it your fault for not fire-bombing the alley while the crack-heads are asleep? If you answered yes to any of these versions of the question you are part of the problem, even if you answered yes to the last one, which <u>will</u> get you my vote for next President of the United States.

5. When Jeremy was walking home from work, listening to his headset one Thursday night he was robbed by two larger young men. Was it his fault for not paying attention or my fault for scheduling him to get off after dark? Mind you, every one that I worked over, with, and under, at this 110-person business blamed Jeremy's mugging either on him, the trusting soul, or on me the heartless slave-driver.

How We Sanction Those Who Hunt Us

The fact is all of these situations are ones I documented in Baltimore, and everyone concerned, even the victims, answered 'yes' to all of the implied questions. This is proof positive that Baltimore is a predation zone; a Hobbesian world where it is considered natural and reasonable to attack anyone who is not vigilant. If we lived in a civilized world, like ancient Lydia, the answers would all be 'No, it is the fault of the attacker and their hand should be shorn from their right arm.'

Yeah, you're probably right. It's more exciting to be a barbarian.

Enjoy the hunt.

James LaFond, 5/18/2012

Living Lost

Honoring A Derided Male Instinct

© 2012 James LaFond

What can former NBA badass Charles Barkley and an aspiring hip-hop artist teach us about self-defense?

A lot, as long as you remember not to listen to your wife when the time comes to practice what I am about to preach. So, as if you could not have guessed, I give you another piece of dubious literature in the 'Don't forget people are predatory primates' self-help-through-disturbing-enlightenment sub-genre.

Charles Barkley

The day after I interviewed a young man about being the target of a violent crime, I saw Charles Barkley perpetuating an 'old wives' tale' and was inspired to write this rebuttal.

Don't Get Boned

'Sir' Charles has recently been making some diet commercials. In one of the TV spots he plays the ugliest transvestite I've ever seen. In a more obscure commercial, he gives lip service to the generations-old American criticism that men are stupid, stubborn and socially inflexible, and that these facts are borne out by the natural reluctance of men to ask for directions when lost. This criticism of American men is so old that it has become a commercial and sitcom cliché.

So, we know what the people who pay NBA players to wear dresses think of the folly of not asking for directions when you are lost. Let us then slide a little ways down the African-American economic ladder for the viewpoint of a local North Baltimore hip-hop artist.

Vagabond

"It was just after dark I'd have to say, spring or summer. Bobby had called me and asked if I wanted to go to a club with him. I was like 'sure' so we decided that I'd meet him over in his neighborhood in Park Heights…

Don't Get Boned

...I got lost so I asked this guy for directions, asked if he knew Bobby. He said sure, he knew Bobby. He said to follow him that it was just one street over. So I follow this guy and he's on his cell phone...

I turn this corner and the next thing I know I see all these people and somebody shoves me. Then I get punched in the head from behind and this dude is saying, "Where you from?"

I said I was just minding my own business and he says, "Oh, so you think you tough?"

Someone grabbed me—I think he came up on me from behind—and I punched. I hit him and he fell. I punched a guy who had a big front [a gold grill].

There was a lot of people. I have no idea how many. It was nice out and there were a lot of people on the street.

I was stayin' on my feet okay with my hands up and this big dude with a hat hit me hard! He hit me so hard I was gone! So they all pulled me toward this brown car. I'm on the ground and they're stompin' me. I was coverin' with my hands and elbows. Then I got hit in the neck and it didn't feel right. You know, I had been getting hit, and this hit just didn't feel right."

Vagabond showed be an inch long half-inch wide scar left from a stitched puncture wound to the left muscle of the neck into cervical vertebrae #2 indicating that the attacker was right-handed. Although he never saw or heard a blade it looks to me from the scar that he was stabbed with a broad-bladed single-edged folder with a deep-wedge cross-section.

"I'm on the ground trying to cover and get up and wrestling with these guys while I'm being stomped. That's when I saw this guy reach over someone who was hitting me. I raised my elbow to cover and he got me in the elbow [*indistinct scar on left elbow on the outside where the tricep and radial muscles attach*]. That's when I figured it was a knife...

...We saw some cops and everybody ran."

This last statement is so important. Vagabond was ruthlessly and opportunistically ambushed and now knew that he was in a fight for his life. However, the last people in the world he thought would help were the police. He ran from the police just like his attackers because, in Baltimore, if you are a young man fighting for your life, there is an even bigger enemy out there, and that enemy is the police.

"I called my mother and made it to this seven-eleven at Mondawmin. There was this guy there about ten years older than me. He looks at me and says, "What happened to you?"

I said, 'I got banked.'

I was goin' to take the bus home. But this guy gave me enough money to get a hack [illegal cab] home. My mom did get me to the hospital and I got stitched up.

You know, I'll never ask for directions again. I didn't realize that askin' for directions was just like sayin' 'Hey I'm alone bank me.'"

Calling out the Hyenas

There are some interesting aspects of urban life illuminated by this young man's story. From a behavioral standpoint it paints a very concise picture of an impulsive ambush.

Vagabond's attackers had only about three minutes to plan and spring their attack.

Of course there is the police-as-ultimate-enemy theme, which is usually present in black-on-black situations.

This does illustrate a rare use of the knife, in that knives are usually used by lone individuals and the stabber, until this, the 318th edged-weapon incident I have documented, has never before stabbed in such a reaching manner. Of course the stabber was reaching over another attacker. Vagabond was also fairly certain, although it was dark and he saw no blade, that the stabber had his index finger extended along the blade.

What is not surprising here is that a lone older man helped the stabbing victim out. The tendency is for groups of bystanders to ignore a stabbing victim, and for individual males, always older than the victim, to help out.

By far, the most salient point to be taking away from Vagabond's story is this: when you ask for directions what you are actually saying is, "I am lost, alone, isolated, and in your power. If you are ever going to attack someone this is probably the best chance you are likely to get."

Don't Get Boned

Remember we are all being hunted every day. Fortunately, like the healthy zebra grazing next to the just-fed lion, we usually fail to make the menu through no fault of the predators we coexist with. When lost, unless at sea or on Everest, I recommend remaining lost. Just make sure you keep moving as if you know exactly where you are going or who you are looking for.

Here's to avoiding the neighborhood welcoming committee.

James LaFond, May 2nd, 2012

Andy Boy

A Profile in Mismanaging Aggression

© 2012 James LaFond

Fortunate Son

You've either known one of these guys, or you have seen him portrayed as a petty movie villain. His daddy was rich and he was spoiled. The world owes him, even though he fears it deeply, and the people beneath him are just pawns in that insecure game of mental chess he plays with himself so that he doesn't have to face the fact that he'll never be the man Daddy was. There is a reason that this seeming caricature of a villain is so common in poorly written movies and modern literature. A guy like this is easy to dislike and easy to write. He and his kind do serve a purpose for those of us who wish to deal with the real problems of life. They provide a cautionary tale for the mismanagement of whatever they are involved in.

The Specialist

I was a temporary supervisor, a specialist who worked for Andy, a feminine type who liked men. I was just there to train his people and get his operation in order, and to leave. The problem with people knowing you are just a trainer, even if you have the authority to terminate them, is that they know that you are going away. The hardcore slackers will hang back and comply, and then tear apart the organization after you leave. But their tactics are passive-aggressive and will take time to corrupt what you built, so there is a long-term benefit to the company. The dysfunctional and disruptive characters thankfully eliminate themselves, except, that is, for the idiot at the top. You can't very well fire him.

Stupid Stan

One morning, in the last two hour stretch of the ten hour night shift, which meant this was 20-hours into my triple-shift work day, we were behind. The doors were opening for food stamp day in two hours, and we had had two callouts, and still had half a trailer of freight on the sales floor.

Don't Get Boned

Stupid Stan was a short muscular dude with cornrows wearing a wife-beater and jean shorts. He came up to me and said he had to leave early so that his mother could go to work. His attendance had been terrible and this would force me to fire him. I explained this to him and he stated that his mother made more money than him and that her job was more important [the guy was 27] so I would have to fire him.

I shook his hand and said, "Okay, you are terminated, no hard feelings."

I was yawning and half asleep as I pulled open the door to let Stan out. As I looked up and pulled the door frame toward my face his fist stopped, Stan having realized just in time that his ill-timed sucker punch was going into impact the heavy metal doorframe. I just laughed and herded him into the lobby with the door and locked it behind him as he glared and said, "You just make me so mad, I want to hit you!"

I retorted, "Sorry. Have a nice day."

I showed the film evidence to Andy when I forwarded Stan's termination paperwork in preparation for the eventual unemployment hearing. Andy looked at me as he froze the video on the frame where Stan's fist stopped just short of the intervening doorframe, "But that was not an attack. He didn't hit you."

I was dumbfounded, "Look if I shoot at you and miss it is still an act of violence. We can use this as proof positive that he was uncooperative on the job."

Andy just didn't get it, did not understand violence. Even after the off-duty cop that worked for him broke up a budding knife fight between a cook and a janitor in the kitchen, he continued to discuss the incident as an argument just because no-one was actually stabbed.

Stupid Stan called and asked for his job back and then said, "I'm sorry about what happened."

I responded, "Is that an apology for your poor attendance, poor work, or inability to sucker punch a sleepwalking man?"

He snapped, "Oh fuck you. I wish I would have hit you."

Long Paul

Long Paul stood six feet and ten inches and was even less intelligent than Stupid Stan.

He was also very lazy and refused to do his assigned work. I had consistent policies that I enforced equally so these guys knew before they came to work when they were getting the ax, even the stupid ones. Paul brought a big scary dreadlocked uncle to intimidate me. I did not want to get ganged up on so I waited for the uncle to leave and then fired Paul, quietly, respectfully, and according to a sport fisherman's catch-and-release ethic.

As I turned to walk away I suddenly felt dizzy. I had a very bad sinus infection at the time and thought I had just turned too quickly and lost my balance. Then I heard my glasses rattling down the aisle for 48 feet behind me to my right. I also noted that my left foot was lifted off the floor and that only my right ear worked.

I set my left foot back down and bent my knees slightly and shrugged my shoulders [acting like I was against the ropes] and turned to face the man that I now realized had hit me. Paul was already five paces toward the door [five of my paces and three of his] and the cashiers were gasping and staring at him and I, stunned by the loud sound of the slap.

My immediate reaction was to call the police to make sure that Paul did not wait outside on the parking lot for my night captain who I did not want being attacked. I talked to the responding officer, retrieved my bent glasses, and began enjoying a life with 60% hearing in the left ear. To this day my left ear always feels over-pressurized. It was a hell of an open-handed hook.

I reported this to Andy, who summed me to a meeting with a police officer that he knew. The police officer said that I should never again terminate an employee alone, that I should have a security witness and a management witness. I agreed that this was standard policy with big companies, but that I had seen the rage this causes in terminated employees, as they are ganged up on, fired by committee, and escorted out by an armed goon. I said, "I've fired thirty-one men, and there have only been two simple attempts at a single strike. It's not like Paul beat me down and stomped me. I'd rather take that chance than humiliate those twenty-nine decent guys who just couldn't make the team. Who knows, you fire a guy like Paul by committee and maybe he comes back with a gun and hoses down the front end?"

Andy sided with the cop, which I understood from a legal liability standpoint. And that is how the cop understood it. This was not a measure to prevent violence, but to inoculate the company against a law suit possibly filed by my sons if I got killed. But Andy thought that ganging up on all of your employees that could not make the team and then humiliating them and treating them like a criminal was going to prevent violence. I shook hands and told the cop I would not fire people alone, and told Andy, that despite his suggestion, I would not fire people over the phone. What I in fact decided, was that I was done firing people. If I could not give a man the courtesy of facing him and letting him go with a 'thank you' for the effort and an offer to counsel him on his job seeking efforts, I would not fire him.

Again though, Andy proved that he was incapable of understanding violence and how it erupts in the mind of the aggressor, often as a feeling of inequity or persecution, warped or not.

Mama's Boy

I was present when Andy Boy's security man collared a female shoplifter and her large 14-year-old son. I was behind him in a supporting role as we walked the two to the back for processing. In these cases the shoplifter is fined $50 plus the value of what they attempted to steal. They are issued with the paper work that summons' them to court. They are then often held for the police at our discretion. The cops will talk to the petty criminal and check to see if there are warrants for their arrest, or perhaps parole or probation conditions that have been violated.

As we walked into the stockroom the boy stopped and mentioned that he had something that he shouldn't have. He then raised his cupped right hand from his belt line, up his centerline and in front and above his right shoulder and said, "Here I keep this with me for defense, take it."

It was a five dollar tactical folding knife with a thumb-post and a butt-spike. The closed knife was not grasped by a single one of the boy's five digits, but just rested in his palm. The butt-spike was not even evident as it rested against his palm. He was offering this concealed weapon up as passively as he could. Granted, this was stupid, as he should have just given verbal indications of his armed status. But he was just a stupid kid, and did not yet realize how terrified cops and security people are of the knife, of any knife.

The security man passed the knife to me as he gagged, then he began having an asthma attack and melting down as he spread-eagled the boy and patted him down as if he were an apprehended terrorist at an airport. I did my best to calm everybody down. The boy was beginning to feel threatened physically and seemed capable of taking the security guy, so I intervened and coached him on how to handle the cops that were coming while I detailed the security guy to take care of Mom.

The cops came and locked up Mom for drugs she had on her and took the boy away to a juvenile detention facility for attempting to stab the security man with the knife. After they left he asked me for a knife combatives lesson in the hall and I explained a few things, particularly the innocent nature of the boy who was trying to do the right thing. He agreed that we did not want to see that victim of bad parenting spending time in a juvenile corrections facility with hardened gang members learning their ways. I filled out his security report because his hands were still shaking.

Andy called me to his office after reviewing the report and berated me for filling out a false report that some 'sleazy defense lawyer' could use to exonerate the savage juvenile delinquent that tried to murder his security man. He tore up the report and swore himself to the civic duty of seeing to the boy's prosecution and incarceration, forbidding me to have anything to do with helping the security man in the future. That was easy enough to agree to in all honesty, because I could not stand to work for Andy Boy another day of my life.

Boy Perfected

Andy Boy is the perfect example of the spoiled, suburban, white-bread elitist coward who claims to want to make things better for society, but in reality is nothing but a spiteful terrified child who will defend against nothing and attack everyone in his power in a vein expression of his fear and frustration. So that Andy Boy could feel like a man, like he wasn't actually somebody that fantasized about being mounted by an alpha male, he did whatever was in his small power to make certain that a boy, who stupidly tried to do the right thing, and with at best half a chance at a decent life, was going to be housed with the worst adolescent monsters our society has produced.

I don't know how that story ended because I left in disgust. I do hope that the 'sleazy defense lawyer' materialized and kept the kid out of the corrections system. Andy Boy is just another example that fear is not a gift, but a curse, the spongy foundation of a rotten overweening society.

Getting Out of Dodge

Assessing the Lethality of Your Habitat--You Wimpy
Little Ape

© 2012 James LaFond

I recently watched both installments of Cocaine
Cowboys, a stunning documentary about the 1980s
drug trade. As I watched the interviews and vintage
news clips, and then considered the title, I was
stricken by how the Old West the 'Wild West' was
constantly invoked to explain the modern
psychopathic drug economy. Then all of the
needling reminders that we were descending back
into the barbarity of those who had 'won the west'
at gunpoint came back. Foremost among them was
my father-in-law's sage advice to 'get out of Dodge';
when the wife was mad.

Curious as to how modern urban violence equates,
if at all, to 19th Century rural frontier violence, I
called Dominick up in Gothom wondering if he had
read about this in any local newspapers. Sure
enough he recommended Robert R. Dykstra's: Field

Notes, Overdosing on Dodge. Satisfied that my opinions were in line with this diligent academic's research, I now felt free to vent my survivalist spleen.

The Ivory Tower, The Dark Tower & The Old West

As could be expected the debate over whether we are more civilized than our hallowed ancestors has been confined to the gun control debate. Excuse me liberal gun-haters and conservative NRA gun-lovers, but gun control does not even belong in the self defense debate. Guns are for the enforcement of social will, the holding of outposts and homesteads from insurgents and raiders, and the protection of property—and for dueling I suppose. If JFK had a python strapped to his hip it would not have saved him. Likewise, the gun used to rob you will be a black market product not subject to gun control legislation.

For example: I recently served as an unarmed escort for three hundred people carrying valuables. Two particular men I walked to the parking lot as I looked for the pack attack goons that normally preyed upon the pencil-necked patrons of these collectable card venues. The men hunting them knew me to be unarmed, as I had ejected them from the venue earlier. After I got these men to the parking area and returned to escort some other event goers, the gunmen emerged from the bushes—literally—and robbed one of the men [the one with the $500 package], failing to get the guy with the $30,000 package, who came and got me.

If I had stayed they would not have approached, as they had had better opportunities.

Likewise if I were armed, and then left, the same thing would have happened.

If I had been armed and stayed, they would have hit someone else on the other side of the venue.

This is after all predation we are talking about, not dating a hillbilly chick and trying to suck up to her dad. If the $500 geek had a tech nine in his book bag, he may well have been shot as he rooted around for it amongst his dice and trading cards. In Old West terms, 'they had the drop on him'. The entire thing boiled down to environmental and behavioral factors. Having a gun is simply one of many possible behavioral factors, not the godlike intervention of Mister Colt that Old West gun geeks so love to evoke. [Jospeph Campbell, in his interview with Bill Moyers in The Power of Myth, did suggest that the modern reverence for firearms is a form of polytheistic death-god worship.]

Mister Dykstra does a good job of pointing out that the Old West was not the blood bath cinema writers and left-wingers would have us believe, and was also not the cooperative paradise free of gun laws that NRA nuts promote. The most telling point is the power of social mythology. Apparently the term 'get out of Dodge' is a euphemism adopted by Vietnam War vets to describe a perilous place best vacated. That place, in the circa 1970 public consciousness, was Dodge City, only because that was the locale chosen for the longest running and most influential TV show in history, Gunsmoke.

Life as a Crunched Number

Some commentators have attempted to quantify and compare the two, the Old West, and whatever our current standout urban hellhole is. It is inevitably apples and oranges. The best example was of a comparison between a year in Miami when it was the per capita murder capital and a year in Dodge City when a single man died in a drunken brawl which escalated into a shooting. According to the use of the FBI's formula of murders per 100,000 one drunk getting shot was indicative of a more violent place in space-time than Miami, which was enjoying such events as strip-mall machine gun battles and mass suburban executions.

The flaw in the method is obvious, even to a statistical moron like me. If one less drug-dealer got killed in Miami it would have theoretically meant nothing, but perhaps a change in the last digit of a broken down statistic. But if the gun-armed drunk had missed back in 19th Century Dodge City, the scene of his behavior would have suddenly become, rather than a gritty Spaghetti western, more like a perfume commercial, or a hallmark movie episode; daisies waiving in the breeze, as grisly bears hug elk, confederate veterans French-kiss union veterans, and rail barons made sure their accountants are paying all of the taxes they owe, even as a Native American paints a billboard with 'welcome to my ancestral homeland and enjoy my wife white man' punctuated by a smiley face...

In 2011 Baltimore finished 9th in the nation for most deadly locale per 100,000. Detroit and Flint Michigan were #2 and #1 respectively. There is your reality hint, in those numbers. All of the top ten were small to mid-sized cities, and the two worst are really a part of the same urban wasteland, literally next door neighbors. Detroit, by the way, has the highest known feral dog population, highest abandoned house count, and the world's only deserted skyscraper! It is where the History Channel filmed Life After People. Now I know where to go for my next vacation!

Baltimore also has a huge number of abandoned houses [over 25,000] and large expanses of urban wastelands. Ask any Thompson's Gazelle, a watering hole is always dangerous, but one that is 'easy to hunt' is more so, because predators are lazy slackers. Heck lions lay around for 20 hours a day. Imagine how the ungulates feel—perhaps they feel like the janitor paying for his meal at Register #3 with hard-earned cash, while the gangsta at Register #4 with the knot roll of bills and gold teeth is buying his Mountain Dew with his girlfriend's baby's mama's EBT card.

Today our law enforcement geeks and talking heads would have us believe that the lethality of our habitat is based solely on a lottery-like concept or our risk of being killed out of a hundred thousand residents who share some form of randomized risk. This is not realistic. Not even an ungulate on the African savanna, about to be featured in a National Geographic snuff flick, would agree with this reasoning, and he has more common sense than most of us!

Busing Tables at the Feast Surreal

The fact is, a zebra's chance of being eaten by lions is not based on how many ungulates are eaten by African predators out of a hundred thousand. His chances are largely subjective, and has as much to do with his characteristics—health, size, isolation, intelligence, speed, stamina—as with the characteristics of those who hunt him.

How dangerous is your habitat?

The first question to ask is, 'How big is my habitat; how much of it do I use; how much should I use?'

The answer, even amongst motorists, is that the typical human living in an urban center does not actually travel any farther while going about their daily business than a primitive villager. Of course you burn a lot of fossil fuel going this way and that, and backtracking, and going through the drive thru at Taco Bell. However, none of this typically takes you, the modern city-dweller, farther away from your home than the 8 miles that can be comfortably strolled two and from the conceptual watering hole by a fit man on a daily basis.

You suburbanites travel a lot farther but not through populated areas, but generally along paved corridors, which in terms of crime might as well be Star Trek transporters. The danger on the highway is other motorists. If you work in the city, begin assessing your risk when you get into town [the philosopher-gazelle's watering hole we might say], and when you get into your bedroom community, where you are a soft high yield prey item.

Rural people have the an entirely different situation that is made both safer in terms of probability of attack, but worse in terms of lethality of attack, then the city-dweller. People don't drive twenty miles to your farm or trailer just to snatch your purse. Country people, I believe, should have guns, because once they have been selected as crime targets it is for keeps. Maybe that is why there is such a dearth of bleeding heart antigun liberal types in rural America.

So, instead of asking, 'What are my chances in a hundred thousand of being murdered this year', take another approach. Ask yourself, 'How many strong-armed robberies, stick-ups, car-jackings, rapes, abductions, home invasions, and smash-and-grabs happen in my neighborhood and my work area?'

'Should I take any additional precautions?'

Most of those murders are casualties in turf battles over illicit drug distribution. Most of those guys getting shot asked for it, and have probably done it to others. The drug-dealer-death-rate does set your environmental stage. However, if you aren't a crack-dealer what you are left with is dealing with the crack-dealer's customer base, who need to rip you off or knock the shit out of you to get their next hit.

Think of your risk in terms of the lethality of your habitat, imagining yourself being the only prey item on the menu. In your mind's eye erase all of the good working people that you encounter in your daily life, which will be the vast majority of them. Then imagine yourself alone, in some scenario where it is only you on the street; and the 3 panhandlers, the creepy guy feeling himself up, the junky looking for a purse to snatch, the crack-dealer, his muscle, his runner, the two drunks, the fat violent screaming maniac in his pickup truck, the kid who borrowed a stolen gun to collect money for the new video game that is coming out next week, the two jerks looking for a girl to rape while they cruise in their mother's SUV, and the three punks looking for an old dude to beat up so that they can relive the experience as they drink their older brother's malt liquor while he is still in prison...

Who of the above is coming for you?

That is all you need to know.

The Adolescent Art

Passive-Aggressive Intimidation: Who, How and Why

© 2012 James LaFond

Yesterday, Wednesday, July 18th, at 12:21 PM I boarded the #55 from Towson over in Loch Raven Village. The bus was half full, with one person taking up one of each double seat. I noticed that, as usual, most people visibility did not want anyone sitting next to them. The yos and hos sprawled across multiple seats and some very ugly mean looking women made certain to pile belonging next to them. Now, in civilized cities like New York, this behavior earns a bus patron a ticket. In Baltimore, there are no transit personnel other then the driver. This driver is now shut in behind a plastic shield against attack, surrounded with cameras and posted warnings against attacking the driver.

In such a situation I must choose to be intimidated or choose to challenge. I do not challenge women, as I still harbor sentiments about them being non-combatants. So I look for the most aggressive yo; a tattooed wannabe gangbanger with I-pod, ear plugs, muscle shirt, and weighing fifty pounds less then that required to actually stand a chance of defeating me in close quarters combat.

As I sit on his bent leg he pulls it in violently and smacks his lips in disgust. I laugh and start loosening my shoulders in case I need to throw some elbows.

The seat in front of us empties and I don't take it. He smacks his lips again.

The seat next to us empties and I don't take it. He shakes his head and twists in his seat.

The seat behind us empties and I don't take it. He smacks his lips and motions that he wants to get up. I step back to let him out and make him squeeze by me to take the rumble seat in the back. He smacks his lips in disgust and I laugh out loud.

He wanted me to get verbally aggressive with him so that he could gather a click from among the other violent youth on the back of the bus. I didn't play his game and he had no functional testicles, so nothing happened.

Don't Get Boned

Now, the day before yesterday, on the other side of Baltimore County, a white yo did the same thing. When I proceeded to sit on his feet, he yanked them out of the way and then apologized. You see, he was alone. He did not have a busload of potential comrades-in-arms and/or witnesses to my aggression.

Back on Saturday I was walking down a sidewalk as three yos approached in muscle shirts, pre-torn pants riding down around their knees, slouch-walking in apparent anger. They were spreading out and winging their elbows to drive a white woman off the sidewalk. I walked up next to her and stepped out in front of them, forcing them to fight or go around. They went around. However, the terrified white women apologized to them. Taking heart from this they circled back around and came towards us.

I shook out my shoulders and started flexing my feet so that I wouldn't shred my old worn-out ankles when I pivoted. I began visualizing an elbow, and promised myself that the first yo who hit the ground would take a leaping two-footed stomp to the head. I wondered absently if this would trash my ankles. This got me excited, so I started flaring my nostrils to get as much oxygen as I could into my increasingly inadequate lungs. At the last moment they veered around the lady's car and went on their way, flexing muscles and chanting about 'hos and bitches' and other laudable values. I helped the lady with her groceries and told her that apologizing to yos was tantamount to begging for violence.

Who Does Not Engage in Passive Aggressive Intimidation?

Men, children, white women and the elderly do not engage in this behavior. This says a lot. The men occupy the top of the aggression food chain, while the terrified hunched-over white women, innocent children and feeble elderly are at the bottom. Based on this profile of the non-perpetrators it is clear to see the motivation behind the behavior on the parts of the perpetrators.

The profile that emerges is of an insecure person in the middle of the food chain who harbors latent feelings of aggression. This type of person is ultimately very dangerous if they do succeed in attacking, because they will only attack as a member of a group, or with the group's support, which would put a male defender in legal liability. It also points to the offenders.

Who Engages in Passive-Aggressive Intimidation?

Youths of both genders and all races, and black women, engage in this behavior. About one third of black women demonstrate passive-aggressive behavior in mass transit situations, whereas most youths do. However, passive-aggressive black women are more likely to attack and more likely to be successful. These situations sometimes escalate. All aggressions against bus drivers are committed by groups of youths, groups of black women, and lone black women. This is essentially low grade aggression that posses primarily a legal liability to healthy adult male passengers who might be forced to defend themselves.

I choose to challenge rather than to be intimidated. The hos and women leave an out for a man, as he can pretend to be acting chivalrously. The yos leave no choice. You challenge their dominance or you bow your head in defeat.

Don't Get Boned

I suggest you choose the lesser of the two evils which best suits you at the time.

Hunting Chumps #1: Ambushing

The First in a Series of Guides on Hands-on Redistribution

© 2012 James LaFond

"Chump (chump), n. 1.*Informal*, a foolish or gullible person"

-Webster's College Dictionary

A Public Service for the Oppressed

I take issue with the incomplete nature of the definition above. It is not a terrible definition, just a misleading one, as it lacks the salient nuance implicit in contemporary usage. You see, in Harm City a chump is 'a person who deserves to be fooled because they are gullible'.

Most chumps feel safest at work and at home. They then get a look of dismay on their face when they find out that most of those targeted for redistribution by so-called criminals are banked near work or home. So Mister Chump, just in case you were in fear of being the object of an incompetent effort at redistribution, I have crafted this career development and social empowerment primer for that victim of oppression lurking on the underside of your cushy life, wondering how he is going to make ends meet. The solution is obvious, by taking what he needs out of your rear end!

That's enough for you, winner of life's lottery, and rightful candidate for hands-on redistribution.

Empowerment Now

...Okay Son, I feel your pain; know what it is to be a poor dude living in an unjust society next door to wimps who seem to have it all. This article is the first in a series of career development efforts on my part. You see, I have made a fortune—to you any way—selling books based on your boneheaded life choices. Being a righteous man, I see no other moral course but to 'give back' to those who have made my literary infamy possible, by educating those like you in the proper use of smarts and force to 'even things out'.

Don't Get Boned

First, forget using a gun. That is five extra years right there. In fact, if you have a gun, sell it to some gangbanger. Let that fool go to prison. You want to use your head and your hands. You're not some dumbass suburban white boy who actually thinks he's going to get away with offing his old lady, and then gets caught. Killing is stupid. Cops are real good at solving murders, especially if it was a chump who got murdered. They have smartass cops just for that. If you just rob people, then they detail the dumbass cops for that. You want the dumbass cops looking for you, not those smartass cops.

Oh yes, one final thing, dress like you have some sense boy. Leave the hood-rat attire at home and dress like some fool that a dude that makes a lot of money sitting on his ass and bossing people around would trust. Speaking of that dude, that rich prick, learn how to talk to people like him. Don't bank his ass. He carries weight; like a set leader in a suit with cops for muscle. Bank the chumps that work for him! By learning how to talk to this dude you will develop your ability to bullshit the cops, and, more importantly, the ability to convince your donors to give you what you want without going through a bunch of shit.

Now, there is a lot more general advice I could give you. But, since that slumlord forced you to eat the lead paint off of his walls when you were a little pain-in-the-ass, I thought I'd respect the implicit limitations and not stress you out.

Ambushing

Powerful animals, such as the tiger, and the extinct smilodon hunt from ambush. This requires cover. If you are bigger than your prey, then make sure you don't go the way of the smilodon, who was discounted at the evolutionary thrift store by the thinning of the lush vegetation he used to hide in. Hunt from cover big boy. Don't let them see your big ass coming until it's too late.

For you runts, you do not have to be big to be an ambush predator, just bigger than your target. Hell, house cats only weigh eight pounds and kick ass from ambush all the time. They just have the good sense not to bank a Doberman. So, don't be a dumbass. Don't bank the human equivalent of that Doberman. Get yourself a poodle. Make sure you can handle your work.

Location, location, location!

Don't Get Boned

Think about where you would build a drive-thru joint to sell fried chicken if you were some plantation-owner-looking-somebody on a red sign. Now, reverse that logic, and go bank people somewhere else. Don't go where people are hungry—they're already pissed. Go to some joint where people buy things that they think a lot about, so that they will be distracted when you approach them—or bank them, depending on your style. Vans, privacy fences, decorative walls, and yard shrubs make good cover. Also, these very same things are owned by people with far more money than your crack-head friends!

The best place to ambush someone is at their home, when they are leaving for work. This requires observation and good instincts. Don't hit people at peak hours. Most people leave their house between 7 and 8:30 AM. Bank that hard working ass-kisser while he heads to the car at 6 AM. The chick still putting her makeup on at 9:30 AM [who is so damn hot her boss lets her come to work late] as she walks to her car is another good target. After 9 AM most residential neighborhoods are basically deserted, especially when it is cold out. People are easier to hit in the morning, so wake your ass up and get to work!

Don't Get Boned

If you just can't sleep it off in time for the mid-morning stragglers, then hit people while they are leaving work after dark. The second best spot to nail them after dark is in retail parking lots. Stay away from house fronts around dinner time.

Your best bet at night is to nail someone who regularly walks through an area coming or going from school or work. I know one particular guy, I'll call Dude. Dude used to date chicks in working class [chump] neighborhoods so that he could scope out chumps walking by their houses. He would dump the girl after he made his hit, trying to synchronize his crime with that moment when he grew bored with that particular girl.

One Friday night Dude seduced a working woman at a bar, drove home with her, did her on the living room floor, then, as she was getting cleaned up upstairs, ordered pizza. When the pizza delivery guy came to the door Dude took the pizza and the driver's change, and made off into the night, to his regular girl's house a few blocks away.

Now, don't expect to be a pimp like that right off the bat. Speaking of which, you want to take an even longer view. You can't be banking people forever, even chumps. Take Dude above. You know, that chick called him back even after he robbed the pizza guy on her porch. He just nailed it again and scooted. The way I see it, that girl would have put up with just about anything. He should have stayed around and tapped more than that ass. Dude could be living right, even getting this girl to front him money so he can play fantasy football at the bar. What I'm saying is, no matter how much we might admire Dude for his style, you need to have an exit strategy—a retirement plan.

While we are speaking of seduction, remember that the corollary tactic for ambushing a mobile man or any chump-of-opportunity is panhandling. Beg your ass off until he reaches into a pocket, then bank him.

Remember Son, do not run, walk to the nearest safe house.

Harm City Handbook #1

How to Profile Yourself as a Violence Target

© 2013 James LaFond

Below is a guide on making realistic threat assessments based on the subjective slice of reality you inhabit, you squemish bipedal primate...

The Triple-Threat Assessment

Begin by examining the local 'crimescape', the violence scene in your neighborhood, your workplace, and the approaches to both, as well as any frequented entertainment or shopping venues. Then, once you have identified the predators in those environments which you frequent, look at yourself in the mirror, as if you were the potential burglar, mugger, stick-up man, rapist or murderer, considering the reflection therein as your potential prey. Next identify your top three most likely aggressors. That is going to cover 98% or your potential threats. Your primary aggressor will probably occupy 60-70% of your actual risk.

What about your wife, your children?

Look, the pedophile that will molest your son is a zero threat to you. He will not even snatch your mother's purse. Our risks are subjective and even interactive. Below are four examples of threat assessments. I have analyzed myself and three subjects of my study who I have interviewed extensively.

Example One: James LaFond & Ja-wan Cool

James is a middle-aged white man. He lives in the city as a writer, and works in the county as a supermarket clerk and a boxing coach, earning less than 12K annually.

Ja-wan is a young black man. He lives in the city as a hip-hop recording artist and performer. He works, with James, in the county as a supermarket clerk, earning less than 12K annually.

James' primary threat is violent groups of black urban youths.

Don't Get Boned

Ja-wan's primary threat is violent groups of black urban youths.

Both of these men have been repeatedly attacked and threatened by young black men with guns, knives, fists, and athletic shoes.

James' secondary threat is being profiled and harassed by suburban cops as he walks to his job site. His civil rights are violated by police officers about once a year.

Ja-wan's secondary threat is being profiled and harassed by city and county cops as he travels to and from work. Ja-wan was once being stabbed by a group of young black men for cutting through their 'hood'. When the police responded, he fled instinctively, along with his attackers, not being able to conceptualize a law officer as a friend, savior or even social arbiter.

Ja-wan is more at risk from cops than James is.

James' tertiary threat is suburban white men in pickup trucks cruising in the county and coming into the city to buy drugs. Such men threaten him with 'recreational' group bonding beatings about once per year.

Ja-wan's tertiary threat is also pairs and trios of suburban white men cruising in pickup trucks.

Since white suburban men are terrified of urban blacks Ja-wan has no fear of attack while in the city. Therefore James has a higher risk from this group than Ja-wan. Note, both individuals fear the police more than the suburban white men based on the fact that police are unbeatable adversaries and cannot be escaped from, as they have helicopters, and, unlike suburban white men, are not afraid of dismounting from their vehicles and aggressively pursuing their quarry in the ghetto.

So, James and Ja-wan share a nearly identical threat profile, which makes perfect sense, as they are both artists living in urban poverty and eking out a living in the very same suburban food market. There overall threat level is identical, rated at probable for annual attacks and monthly threats. This also makes sense, since the only thing differentiating them is age and ancestry.

The best possible survival plan for these two is to travel together. This will eliminate their primary and secondary threats. Cops harass James and Ja-wan in different settings, and black urban youths harass and attack them for different reasons.

Therefore they can inoculate one another from these threats by their very presence. This strategy also places them at a numerical parity with their shared tertiary threat, the white suburban male in his pickup truck.

Example Two: Nikki & Shynoah

NIkki is a petite curvaceous young white woman. She lives in an upscale county enclave and works for a Fortune 500 corporation in the county, in collections.

Shynoah is a petite athletic black youth. He lives in the South East Baltimore ghetto and works for a local gang 'set' collecting [you might say that he also works in collections] cash on a side-street for crack cocaine that will be picked up in a back alley.

Nikki is a member of the second-most hunted and second-most murdered demographic in America. Her primary threat is from lone men of her own race, either an estranged mate, or a serial killer.

Shynoah is a member of the most-hunted and most-murdered demographic in our society. His primary threat is from a lone man of his own race, probably an assassin.

Shynoah has a geometrically more likely risk of attack than Nikki. However, once selected, Nikki has nearly zero chance of escaping with her life. Shynoah, with his more practical footwear and attire, finely honed survival instincts, and athletic ability, may very well be able to make it to the emergency rooms with a few rounds 'in his ass' and at least live out his days in a wheel chair. On the other hand, once attacked, Nikki's body might never be found.

Nikki's secondary threat is rape. [Mind you, half of the primary threat group who kill her will rape her first. So this secondary threat is the 'rape and release' scenario.] She will most likely be abducted by an adult male, race variable, and then raped by the same man.

Shynoah's secondary threat comes from police officers, who will arrest him as a team, making his chances of escape as unlikely as Nikki's. He will then be incarcerated in a juvenile detention setting or adult facility. In either case he is subject to rape, beatings and murder at the hands of larger inmates.

Shynoah is more likely to be abducted than Nikki. However, not being so isolated and considered to be an anatomically incorrect victim by most sexual predators, he is less likely to be raped.

Nikki's tertiary threat is to be beaten by her boyfriend.

Shynoah's tertiary threat is to be beaten by his handler.

Nikki and Shynoah also share a fourth threat, nearly as likely as the third. They are both fairly likely to be robbed. Nikki will probably just have her purse snatched. Shynoah will probably be held up at gunpoint.

Nikki profiles for a threat a decade [such as an invitation to give her a lift tendered by a strange man]. Any of these 'threat situations' could be lethal. If Nikki just gave up her job and hitchhiked across the country she would probably not make it to the Pacific Ocean.

Shynoah profiles for a threat a day, one potentially lethal threat situation per week, and one murder attempt or laid ambush per year. If he just gave up his job and hitchhiked across the country he would be far better off.

Although their threats are very similar, if of a far different 'social texture', they can be addressed by lifestyle changes more easily by Shynoah than Nikki. Shynoah is pretty much volunteering for all of this peril. Nikki was born to it. If Shynoah declines to move out of town and get a real job then he just needs to concentrate on honing his behavioral and physical survival skills.

Nikki, though a less likely target than Shynoah, is a far softer one, and must absolutely conduct a thorough assessment of her risks, and practice behavioral self-defense [such as James' and Jawan's buddy system above] with vigilance. If she does not, than her self-defense strategy, if any, amounts to rolling two dice twice every time she walks out the door, and hoping she doesn't hit box cars on both die-casts.

Conclusion

For most people that metaphorical 'die roll'; the perceived safety of hiding within a massive population like some ungulate munching grass amidst the herd while the wolves circle, is the extent of their plan for survival and maintaining their personal autonomy. That is the portion of the self-defense problem that can be addressed by each and every individual, every day of their circumscribed lives.

You might ultimately decide that survival is not worth the effort of moderating your behavior according to your own subjective threat pyramid. But you will not know until you have made the assessment.

Harm City Handbook #2

Justifiable Armed Defense in Public Spaces

© 2013 James LaFond

Justifiable is the key concept here. What it means is that you can honestly justify breaking the law when questioned by the cops, persecuted by the Municipal lawyers, and eventually sued by the ambulance-chasing scum-suckers that will rise from the bowels of our corrupt society to avenge the criminals who threatened, attacked or attempted to kill, you. This article will not employ legal terminology as I am not qualified to define it.

The Darwinian Facts

You will be attacked by a bigger, or younger, or stronger, or more numerous, and possibly armed, aggressor. Your best bet in terms of immediate survival is weapon use. This will, however, always mean you are breaking the law. If someone tries to kill you and you injure them, then you have both broken the law. And if you are some big karate guy don't think that the responding cop is going to feel any better about the fact that you could have kicked his ass too.

What you and your lawyer have to do in court—and this begins being spun at the scene when you talk to the meathead cop while he misspells everything you say—is prove that you were compelled to break the law in order to survive, and should therefore be excused. In the eyes of the government it is never okay to injure or kill. Even cops have to go through this process of justifying their actions when they use force. Below I offer some tips on making your actions as defensible as possible.

The Salient Points

1. If you produce a body you will do time with some even more dangerous bodies.

2. If you use a purpose-built weapon [gun, knife, RPG, etc.] to defend yourself, even if just by brandishing it, you will lose that weapon and probably do time.

3. If you use an improvised weapon which you have crafted or altered [like a whipstick], or some kind of outlawed weapon like a double-edged dagger or martial arts flail, you will lose the weapon and most likely do time. You cannot even carry this stuff without the danger of being locked up.

4. If you hurt anyone, in any way, in any manner, you can reasonably expect do time or be sued.

5. If you do not kiss the responding officer's ass things will not go well.

6. You do not have any right to defend your property with force. You cannot injure or kill a mugger or purse-snatcher to prevent the theft of, or to recover, your goods.

7. You must be able to prove that you were in fear for your life or limb, that you had no other option like running or driving away, and that you used the minimal amount of force necessary to insure your survival.

8. Your attackers just have to make certain they lie consistently, unlike your sorry self, who must present facts and back them up. The crooks are

basically just composing a self-serving rap and you are writing a term paper with your guts.

Example

I used to carry swords, knives and even guns, to protect myself. Do you realize what a high-stress pain-in-the-ass that is? If you get caught, you go to jail. If you get attacked and defend yourself you go to jail. It is a lose/lose situation.

This time last winter, in February 2012, I fell asleep on the bus and missed my stop, waking up at the major transfer point. Instead of walking home through backstreets past grannies letting out their dogs and old dudes waiving good morning, I was hoofing it up the main drag; all but deserted, ghetto barbers just flipping their closed signs around to open. As I walked through my majority black neighborhood's business district three of my own kind, lowdown white-trashians, in their mid thirties, emerged from a dive just ahead of me.

The bearded leader and the big dude nodded at each other and spread out so they would have my flanks when I shouldered my way past their drunken friend. I was groggy, and had to cross the street anyhow, so crossed before we met. They took this as a sign of weakness, and huddled up, looking at me all the while. They then changed direction, crossed the street behind me, and began trailing me. I was an obvious working guy getting off a bus on Saturday morning, and I suppose they smelled the payout in my pocket.

I am accustomed to being threatened by young blacks, suburban rednecks cruising in pickup trucks, and cops. I have well-worn survival responses to these aggressors. But this, fellow urban palefaces blatantly hunting me, this threw me off my game. I became angry and glared over my shoulder at them as I picked up my pace. Beard and Big-boy touched hands to shoulders, nodded, and herded their portable casualty with them. I nodded to them to follow, knowing now that it was clearly on, and decided to take out the witless little drunk first, so that he could not serve as a witness.

I was armed with an ink pen and a case-cutter. This was a problem. The ink pen is a one-shot weapon and has to be driven into the eye or throat, which, could be twisted around by Beard's lawyer as an indication of lethal intent. We were all wearing coats, so I would have to use the razor to slice balls, hands, throats and faces. Hand slashes could be argued as defensive wounds incurred by the three poor drunks I had tried to individual-up on. The throat is possibly lethal and the balls and face could bring maiming charges. The thighs would just make a lot of blood, and these guys may have been heroin users, considering the locale. I would only use the razor if they followed me all the way to my apartment steps before attacking.

There was an outpost of utility in this sea of barbarity, between my anxious self and my humble abode. Deals, the local dollar store was a regular shopping spot of mine, and was just ahead. I made for the dollar store and left them clustering on the lot, planning my ambush. When I entered the 70-year-old lady at the register told me I had to lay my bag down on the register before shopping. I responded, "I have three guys following me. I'm not trusting you with my bag."

I had the manuscript for by This Axe!, $5 in change, a borrowed DVD, my work gloves, and my toothbrush and such. These guys were not even welcome to my toothbrush. I went back into the canned good aisle to arm up. My preferred flail head was not present, so I bought a can of pumpkin pie filling, asked for an extra bag, and headed out to meet my foes.

Don't Get Boned

When I emerged onto the walk—having the high ground I might add—I twirled my just-made food flail and grinned. And yes Adam, I did experience that inappropriate response [This is PG14. If you want to know the inappropriate response to this type of thing that sometimes plagues me, you will have to read When You're Food: Mara Chrismass Yo.] Beard shook his head sideways at Big-boy's inquiring gesture, and they headed back down to the bar they had crawled out of.

Now, in a pinch, using a work tool as a weapon, provided you are on your way to or from work, is defensible. However, something as nasty as a razor will turn prosecuting heads. You don't want that. On the other hand, defending yourself with a grocery you have just purchased, the receipt for which is in your hand to match the time of your attack on these innocent pedestrians, is even more defensible. Additionally, it is not an edged weapon, and edged weapon use is really taboo in our sniveling society.

If you are being followed duck into a liquor store and buy a bottle—try to find a long neck, and use it as a club on the first dude and a knife on the second. Hardware stores were once ideal, but now largely gone. Food stores are ubiquitous, and dollar stores in particular carry an array of cheap canned goods which is what you want.

Building the Food Flail

Make sure the clerk double bags your single can order. If the bags are cheap get a third bag.

Do not use cans with beveled bottoms, but with rims on top and bottom.

Do not use zip-top cans.

Use cans with some product density. The contents should not slosh when you shake them. I recommend: sweetened condensed milk; pumpkin; tomato paste; cranberry sauce; corned beef or frozen rolled meat. If it is just a farm store, find a glass-bottled beverage.

Beware that cans over a pound in weight will rip through the bag, and are just one-shot flail heads. Ideally you want a 14 ounce can of sweetened condensed milk.

Tactics

Don't be a jerk like I was that morning making a lariat out of the bag like it was a battleaxe and getting warmed up for battle like Mel Gibson just told me I was a hero. Be sneaky. Hold your flail low to the side and point the finger of your other hand in their face—or use the palm. Just get their attention with your left hand before you whip that can of calories into the side of their head. Target the side of the head as this attacks the equilibrium and is thinner and easier to cave in than the top and front. Facial attacks only work against wimps. Truly tough guys can handle any facial trauma short of eye removal and keep coming.

Once the enemy is down, you may not justifiably continue to beat them unless they are armed and able. I recommend stomping the ankles if they are unarmed and dangerous. Never stomp the head unless they are armed and deadly.

If the attacker was part of a group make sure you injure them all, so that none can claim witness status.

Do not run. Call the cops and start spinning the story your way to the 911 dispatcher.

Don't Get Boned

When the cop gets there, you must not be a chest-thumping righteous defender of your liberty, but a reluctant traumatized defender, who, above all, is an ass-kissing machine! Be a car salesman on Presidents Day when your fearless defender rolls up in his cruiser. Make sure you are holding what is left of your grocery order as if it is the precious delicacy you would have prepared for your wife and kids, and your gay-activist uncle who sings Bob Dylan songs at Green Peace rallies—"If only this would not have happened officer. Oh God, my life will never be the same!"

Bury the beast until you get home. Then you can carve another notch on the pantry doorframe and watch Brave Heart one last time.

Harm City Handbook #3

Justifiable Armed Home Defense: Firearms & External Property

© 2013 James LaFond

I have had numerous recent requests for advice on home defense. In this article I will speak largely from experience as someone who has managed to ward off numerous attempts by criminals to gain entry by force into my home or a place of business I was charged with defending. By no means am I an expert on this subject. However, I've held off aggressors at my own front door with blades, extension weapons and firearms. So take this experience-based advice and find some apocalypse pantry author online who specializes in domestic security tactics and combine these information resources to fit your needs.

For instance, if you are a rancher near Juarez, it is already the End of Days and past time to work out your fields of fire. But if you are Joe Bohemian grooving in your ghetto flat, law enforcement's concern with making certain you are harmless to cops—and hence to criminals—and municipal statutes intended to discourage gangland firearms use will hinder your ability to effectively defend yourself without putting yourself at grave legal risk.

The Firearms Choice

Most people, when they think of home defense, think of firearms. I do not. Firstly, this is because I am not qualified with any firearms and have never been a decent shot as my hands have always been unusually shaky. My bother, the best shot in his company in the 82nd Airborne, once hit me and cussed me out at a firing range for embarrassing him in front of the assembled rednecks when I missed by unthinkable margins.

The other reason why I have no desire to employ firearms is because any use of a firearm, particularly in an urban municipality, will immediately bring legal heat, even if you are a cop. I'd rather fight a gang of home invaders with my gladius and cargo-hook than be persecuted by lawyers that spent eight years and a small fortune to learn how to get me convicted.

Don't Get Boned

When I was a nut-job urban survivalist being threatened by armed criminals on a daily basis in the mid-1990s, I did carry a 20-gauge shotgun on the street on two occasions, and also totted an illegally modified carbine. The stress was too much though. I calculated that I was more likely to become the workload of some cop who was just trying to do his job than to draw down on a street thug. I got rid of my firearms in 1999, preferring the possibility of becoming nothing but a knife wielding meat-shield when my house got overrun, to the stress of repeatedly breaking such a taboo law.

To begin with, I never liked the idea of using my guns for home defense and instead used them as portable deterrents on the street and to drive invaders off my property before they entered the house. Once my oldest son was a teenager I would not even consider using a firearm for home defense because of the possibility of popping him or a friend coming home late at night. There was also the example of the local business owner who shot at an armed robber only to have the slug pass through the wall and kill the pizza maker next door.

Again, as an able bodied man, I saw no reason to take a chance on one of my bullets taking out one of my family in another room. I once roomed with a guy who was walking back upstairs, all shaken up after he had repelled a home invader with his .22 caliber magnum revolver at the front door while I was loading my twenty gauge with buckshot upstairs. On the way up the stairs, his jittery legs locked up and he tripped, discharging the gun and almost killing our cat, who literally flew across the room in a ball of furry fright.

I gave my guns away, and committed myself to the home defense course of taking a bullet while I ran someone through. A terrible marksmen I might be, but I still take out young knife fighters with a five-foot pronated lunge on occasion—in fact did it last night. The house I live in is a maze of corridors, doorways and small rooms, perfect for big blades. The belief that a blade can't work against a gun in close quarters is just like the 1970s karate belief that punching can't work against kicking and grappling can't work against punching. You just need to be willing to pay the price to get into your range. When I was 18 I saw news footage of one of Anwar Sadat's assassins being run through with a parade sword—much to my grandfather's delight—and I was sold.

But that is all just my personal preference; my home defense bias. Your situation, perhaps a rural location, squeamishness, an infirmity, or the fact that you are female, might call for a firearm. In such a case I can give no technical advice, only half-baked bias. But there is no shortage of gun-nuts to aid you if you choose that course.

Keep in mind, that whatever weapon you choose for home defense, that its use carries an inherent legal liability.

The External Property

You have no right in most municipalities to use any force beyond control grappling to protect your property. If you are outside of your car and someone is trying to break in, and you do the same thing to them with a tire-iron that they are doing to your car window with that flashlight than you have committed a violent crime, and they have only committed a property crime. If you have a child or spouse in the car, then you can claim to have been going to their rescue, but will be called upon to prove it. Also, if you are in the car, you may claim that you thought you were defending against a carjacking or kidnapping and try to justify your use of force that way.

Don't Get Boned

Do not advance from your house to meet an aggressor unless you are doing so to protect a child, spouse or other dependent who is outside. In 2002 I was in my living room waiting for my son to come home from school while I taped up a sparring stick. I heard the sound of a foot pursuit nearing the house, so darted outside with the stick in hand in nothing but a pair of cut off jeans. As I emerged my son and his friend were leaping headfirst over the fence as four older boys pursued them. I leaped the fence to meet the attack just as one of the boys hit the fence and pushed away, mumbling to the other aggressors, "Shit, yo, fuckin' Tarzan en shit!"

I paced up and down the sidewalk until they were out of sight, while my son rooted in the shed and found a steel pipe in case he needed to reinforce me. My actions may seem justified but could have gotten me in big trouble. If cops would have showed up then I might have been arrested. If I had hit one of those kids with that stick I would have been charged. At that time I was working in the city at night before coming back out to this suburban peninsula, and had brought that combative ghetto mentality home with me. I crossed the line when I hopped the fence. If my son and his friend had made it inside I would have crossed that legal liability line when I left the house.

You may not defend property. If you have no dependents in the yard or driveway you must retreat into the house, and may not advance from it except at great legal peril.

Hunting Chumps #2

The Virtues of a Slow Wingman

© 2013 James LaFond

I'm sorry Yo. I know I promised my hood-rat readers early this year that I would come through with regular installments to aid yo in the cause of righteous redistribution of The Man's ill-gotten gains into yo lonely pockets. All I can say is, 'yo get what yo pay for homeboy...'

For illustrative purposes I shall be paraphrasing the text of a New York Post article from May 12th 2013 by Natasha Velez—Yo, Yo! Pay attention Yo. Do yoself a favor, and for however many minutes or hours it takes yo to read this heartfelt advice from me to Yo, stop wondering what a New Yor-Rican/Russian babe looks like...

Charles Hackett, a hard working thug, was working the Bronx; just his little corner of it. He wasn't selling drugs to kids—none of that. Charles and his wingman were working East Tremont Avenue near Southern Boulevard at 12:35 pm. Now, I hope I don't need to tell yo that that 'pm' should have been an 'am', feel me Yo?

Okay, Charles and his wingman spot this old fool walking down the street with Mother's Day flowers, a day early. Now an ass-kisser like this deserves to get banked to begin with. And on top of that, Charles spots him flashing a Gold pendent on a chain. From here on out I will be illustrating Charles Hackett's failure to follow established Chump Banking Protocol.

Charles and his wingman walk up on the chump, who is unbelievably old, like a hundred or something, and demand the pendent. The old dude must have been somebody back in the day so he stepped up and fought. They knocked the chump around and took the chain and pendent from his neck. It is always a mistake to fight in broad daylight—to fight at all really. This old dude was walking with some flowers so yo could expect him to step up; and now yo have a fight. Fights are not good for business.

The worst thing Charles did was ignore those two dirt-bags up the street—who turned out to be narcs! So here it comes Yo: yo worst nightmare: old dude flexing in yo face; and fiends morphing into Five-O! Now, yo thinking of course, that that has got to be the worst of it, right?

Wrong! Charles' wingman was faster than him Yo! Now, that dude is so fast they didn't even get his name! But there lay Charles, narc knees in his ribs, hands behind his back, and some hot-ass Russo-Rican babe writing about how he is a creep for beating up some 78-year-old dude who was buying flowers for his deceased wife's memorial photo.

So Yo, this is yo checklist:

1. Do it in the dark

2. Bank chumps, do not fight them

3. Do not do yo work in front of dope-fiends who inexplicably have legs like A-Rod!

4. Do yo work with a slow dude, at least slower than yo fool!!

That is all the advice I have for yo now Yo. Remember, nighttime is yo friend.

It's Unlocked!

Vigilance versus Complacence

© 2013 James LaFond

Think of the most dangerous fighter on the planet: the current UFC champion, whoever he is.

Imagine you—whoever you are—walking down the street next to him in a beanie hat, pink pajamas and yellow slippers with a baby bottle full of formula, sucking away, holding out a diaper to passersby in hopes that some Good Samaritan might change your diaper in a doorway.

Which one of you gets mugged first?

Okay, the ultimate fighter, scary looking mutant jock that he is—only gets mugged by an armed gang, a squad of coked up college ball players, or a hood-rat with a pistol; and then only if he is drunk, obviously distracted and flush with cash, or with a woman.

Don't Get Boned

You, in your cartoon infant getup, are obviously insane and therefore safe even from aborigine headhunters! Nobody mugs the clearly insane if they can help it; and even fewer want to change adult diapers.

Okay, now sit that dangerous man down in a car, in the driver's seat or passenger's seat. Hire a 15-year-old ghetto girl to kill him. Give her an empty wallet and a straight razor—or give her brother a UNICEF envelope and a brick. Either way, for 500 bucks any 15-year-old hood-rat or ghetto girl could turn this stud into a draining piece of meat in seconds...if he is sitting on his butt.

I spend my life passing between the ghetto and suburbia, from a predation zone that everyone knows is a predation zone, to an artificial paradise. Although the numbers pale in comparison to ghetto stats, every major suburban sprawl has multiple violent felonies per a day. Yet all of the suburbanites I know, exhibit a total lack of vigilance when in suburbia, making them an absolutely doable deed if anyone decides to prey upon them. Then when they go into the city they prance nervously about, their fear on display; or walk blindly about, unaware, once again an inviting target. There are so many of these easy marks out there, that your typical suburbanite will, like zebra on the savannah, wander aimlessly through life without being targeted. But, on those occasions when they are targeted, these people are already a done deal. There is no self-defense.

I do not believe in self-defense.

I do not believe in justice.

I am a survivor, and I believe in vigilance. My sense of vigilance makes me incompatible with society. Let me give you a typical example of how the over-weaned comfort-craving slaves of our consumer economy always react when I behave rationally, vigilantly. The following happens virtually every time I get into a vehicle with any female, and every time I first get into a vehicle with a man. If some person is nice enough to give this old pedestrian a lift I think the least I can do is look out for them. Why, I am already looking out for myself. It requires no extra effort to look out for them, so I do.

In our culture the vehicle is our mighty chariot, our badge of nobility, a projection of our environmental superiority. People who drive assume the position of power, and often argue with and threaten other motorists when they would never get confrontational on foot. Conversely, they usually show great courtesy to pedestrians, who they assume are totally harmless potential victims of their driving. As a non-driver I find no end to the fascinating observance of the completely irrational behavior of many motorists. Civilian vehicles offer a sense of power where this is none. Consider that even commanders of main battle tanks are reluctant to enter an urban environment without accompanying infantry support.

As an obsolete relic, whenever driving with ladies, I shut everyone into their seat, and then go to my door and shut myself in. I do not shut myself in until I note that no fit male is within a five second walk. Some females take great offense to this; the young lady that drove me into town on her way to work this morning for instance. This morning we were in Utopia. Knowing better than to hold her door for her, I just stood and watched the service man across the street to make sure he was a service man, and not just someone casing her house for burglary. If I thought he was a criminal I would have a talk with him about my primeval belief system; the fact that I worship Woden, etc.

As she fussed with her vehicle and all of her dainty nic nacs, and enough supplies and equipage to get her through a work day and me through a hazardous ordeal in Antarctica, she became angry that I would not take my seat at the very first possible second. Any sane person on this planet would always sit as soon as possible, right? This is what our society believes, that comfort and coziness and a fetal lifeway are the only true universal good. I can't blame her. But, I have told her that I will not sit until I am sure there is not a potential combatant within five seconds. She knows this but a battle of wills ensues as she insists that I take a comforting seat before she gets in. I stand, and stand, and stand. Eventually, thinking me insane, she gets in, perhaps wondering if I have been punched in the head too many times.

The most awesome human killing machine on our planet—Navy SEAL or Anderson Silva—sitting in a passenger seat, is nothing but meat waiting to bleed; a skull ready to cave in, a throat ready to gush.

I am sure you all think I'm crazy. But consider this: I know that I will not be taken unawares unless hunted by a professional assassin—and I don't rate that compliment. You, on the other hand, sliding into your artificial rolling uterus as soon as humanly possible, without even a look around, and making no effort whatsoever to safeguard yourself, your property, your family, and burning perhaps one calorie less than I, have actually invited an attack: a carjacking, a mugging, a hold up. I know a former torturer—a man who trained army intelligence officers in how to torture Vietnamese soldiers at a Maryland military base [where, he claimed, they actually tortured and killed POWs in the 1960's and 70's] who was robbed at gunpoint by a 'ten-year-old kid' as he sat in his car. If it can happen to him, it can happen to you. Sit the UFC heavyweight champion on his ass, and I will find a 15-year-old that could brick his head in where he sits.

Why ask for it?

Why not be vigilant?

Because you are meant to be socio-economic food, raised on a 300-million-person cattle farm to feed whoever is hungry. If, by ill-luck it is your turn to win the lottery of suburban crime, or the higher stakes urban game, your misfortune; that you begged for—were indeed conditioned to invite by reliance on our police state—will serve our masters in the form of more calls for increased police protection; accelerated erosion of civil liberties;

more monitoring of the life you are supposed to believe is private.

I don't believe in advocacy. And, aside from looking out for friends, family and readers I encourage the trend toward people-farming. The more mindless potential victims are wandering about out there, convinced of the armored invincibility of their chariot or the sanctity of their couch, the greater are the chances that I will not be targeted; that there will always be a softer target for the criminals to prey upon.

Remember, when seated—indeed whenever you are comfortable—you are out of danger, your place of comfort assured by others, who will surely be there to protect you if the need ever arises.

The Ethics of Stomping

The Violent Creed of a Cowardly New World

© 2013 James LaFond

I have been nibbling around this subject in Harm City, Modern Combat, and on the Blog. Finally, I have come across a recent network broadcast seen in a late night diner that will provide a point of departure into the darker corner of my mind. This subject is, by the way, the centerpiece of my fiction, where I really wrestle with it from opposing and neutral viewpoints. This subject is the ethics and actualities of group versus individual violence.

The News Story

In some corner of the U.S., lost in the din of the diner as my attention was garnered by the talking head, a 'peewee' football game played out with parents on the sidelines. One boy scored a touchdown for his team, whereupon two boys from the opposing team knocked him to the ground and began kicking him in the helmet. Two of these kicks landed solidly. The victim's mother went ballistic and the story progressed to the interview and commentary stage. I am certain that no criminal charges will be brought, as children at such an age are incapable of such actions.

Soft Little Jimmy

None of this surprised me. From age 6-11 I was consistently chased, grappled, beaten, humiliated, made to make fun of myself, made to cry, and made to declare older teenage boys my master as my face was pressed into the wire fencing to a yard in back alleys in Loch Raven Village, Baltimore County. One of these tormentors was a man-sized polish teenager who delivered papers for the News American, while I delivered papers for the Sun.

My cousin Fred, a big athlete 4 years my senior, did his best to toughen me up for such encounters. I was, not, however inclined to athletics or violence, being just a dreamy and not-so-bright little boy. Therefore I perceived Fred's hours of anatomical pretzel-making with me as the raw dough on various grass and carpeted surfaces to be just more painfully heaped humiliation. Although I was not the brightest kid around—I was the brightest kid in my special education class—I quickly discerned two violence templates: the lone terrifying domination by an unbeatable individual; and the lonely confusing domination by a cohesive group, the individual components of which had at least one thing in common, their disapproval and victimization of me.

I was enrolled in football and baseball, I think, to help bring me out of my reclusive shell. I spent my football games on the sideline and the baseball games swatting gnats in left field and striking out. After practice I saw plenty of action, when my teammates would knock me to the ground, place their knees in my soft belly, slap me, punch me, and tell me I was worthless until I agreed.

This continued until I hit an early and most aggressive puberty.

Scary Jimmy

At age 14 I was boxing at the YMCA and hanging out with my friend Rick, who played fullback on my brother's soccer team. My brother and I did not get along, largely because he was a star athlete. Helping him practice playing soccer in the backyard was an exercise in humiliation as he would dribble the ball through my legs and bounce around like an evil untouchable pixie from some South American nation. My brother was also smarter, better looking and far more popular then I, a 143 pound whack job who trained into the middle of the night fantasizing about crippling grown men in fights in front of their crying families.

I did have some status though, boys as old as 18 feared me. I was a psycho who would stop at nothing to avenge even the slightest insult, and actually snarled like an animal when I attacked people. I had decided when I hit puberty, that I would not justify the actions of those groups who had picked on and humiliated me, by joining one. But that I would become what they feared; that which caused them to band together into groups; a lone predator, someone who savored the whimpering of the enemies they beat into submission. I was a problem child.

Certainly, as a member of the middle school football team and brother to a soccer star [who would go on to become the second highest scoring varsity soccer player in Pennsylvania at only 75 pounds!] some coach or educator would rescue me from myself.

Coach Archie

One day, as I walked through the mall with my friend Rick we ran into coach Archie, also a teacher at the local high school. Coach wanted to speak with me about playing soccer. I responded that I boxed. He reminded me that black men dominated that sport with small brains snuggly protected within massive impenetrable skulls, and that I should involve myself in a white man's sport, and not football, sport of trailer park idiots, but soccer, sport of cultured Europe.

I admitted to being a terrible soccer player. He admitted to knowing this, and tried to recruit me as an 'enforcer'. Coach informed me that he only had one good fighter on the team and he would always be detailed to protect my loud-mouthed hard-charging brother who intentionally drew fouls to get penalty shots and was the likely target of 'side-lining' attempts by 'enforcers' from the other teams. My job would be to stay on the sidelines and go out on the field whenever my brother's behavior would ignite a brawl. I was then to eliminate my counterpart and 'side-line' [not kill, just cripple] my brother's counterpart.

The animal I had become wanted this like a contender wanted a title belt, like a virgin wanted a lover. But the nerd within, Soft Little Jimmy, was still there; someone I still had to live with before I went to sleep at night. I declined, henceforth being an enigma to this man, who observed me stabbing a classmate on my first day of high school and said nothing, and even discussed me as a psychopath of interest openly in advanced placement history class, after seeing me playing dodge ball. Years later when news came that I had hospitalized and nearly killed a friend for beating up my brother, he was likely sad that I had declined a position as his 'enforcer'.

By the age of 16 I knew the reputation of football players as gang rapists to be well-deserved, and also knew them to be cowards when alone. As a welterweight boxer of no great ability I reveled in the potent ego-rush that I got whenever I bumped into a lone football player twice my size and glared into his eyes with barely caged homicidal fury as his sniveling soul tried to escape his impotent bucket of muscle through his belly and found itself cornered there.

A Primal Mirror

I have never been surprised since to hear tales of football players ganging up on individuals and beating them. The tales of European soccer hooligans running wild have never seemed anything but predictable to me. In my heart I have always known that team sports build group courage and erode individual courage. As a researcher and writer I have come to believe that this is deliberate. While the primary purpose of sports on a social level is to draw the critical eye of the masses away from their leaders, and into a fantastical realm of intense though contrived human drama, the purpose of team sports for eroding ones' individuality and cultivating a sense of shared aggression, is very important to the coercive institutions of a hierarchal society.

On my first day of first grade I was crossing Putty Hill and Loch Raven Boulevard to Immaculate Heart of Mary to attend this benign religious institution's elementary school. This was a long diagonal crossing. To my child's eyes it was like crossing the Red Sea. I only have one other memory of this anxious crossing. I do not think it was the same day. I recall looking back as I made it to the far side. The cars would often wait for slower children after the crossing light had changed, but this was purely voluntary. A tall older girl had dropped her binder and the pages began flying around. She was on her hands and knees cleaning them up as the cars waited [today she would be run over I think] and I stood, too enthralled to turn away, too afraid to go back and help.

Soft, Cowardly Little Jimmy.

At this very spot, on my first day of first grade, I looked ahead at three adolescent trees that had some partially installed wire fencing around them where the school lot met the sidewalk before the yield. I began to walk through and was promptly attacked by three second graders who hit me, pushed me down, and kicked me. I remember bouncing off of the rolled fencing. Then came Chris, a big loud-mouthed third-grader, pushing them off of me. Chris became my only friend for years, and ever after that incident I never wanted to be part of a group enterprise—and still loathe the idea—but wanted to emulate Chris, a lone actor in a world of violent group activities.

Today I coach a boxer and a seven-person stick-fighting team out of a karate school two blocks past this very spot. I look twice a week at these trees that are now mature as I walk by. I admire the neat shrubbery that the fencing I had been bounced off of was being installed to protect 44 years ago. As part of a team of individual combatants I feel like I have avoided the fate of the shrubs and the boys that attacked me; that I have turned out more like Chris, wherever he may be.

On Stomping

I am involved as a combat weaponry and 'hands' expert for various martial arts programs. I write widely on the subject. It strikes me as odd that the self-defense aspects of all of these programs focus on the lone attacker. It is not really odd, as our primal fear is of the lone attacker; the cat that stalked our primitive forefathers as they came down out of the trees. This is, however, totally at odds with our current tribal reality. Fights between individuals outside of a sporting context are so rare in our society that I find myself searching for their occurrence like an anthropologist searching for evidence that a lost language is still sporadically spoken.

Virtually all violence is initiated by members of a hostile group against individuals. The balance is group on group. The primary instinctive concern with all of these actions involves putting the target on the ground and then kicking and stomping. Thirty years ago this behavior was only exhibited to any notable degree by members of violent white gangs. It is now Universal American Behavior.

During this same period football has overtaken baseball as the national past time and boxing has fallen away to an archaic exhibition. Boxing, the sport that denies the dominant actor the opportunity to stand over and beat a downed opponent, has been all but replaced by MMA, where beating a downed opponent is trained for.

Does the fading of non-violent baseball and the rigidly limited violence of boxing, in favor of hyper-aggressive football and the more 'realistic' violence of MMA represent art imitating reality?

Could it be that the reality of street attacks being virtually all group actions focused on downing and kicking targets represent reality imitating these combat arts?

Or, are both of these trends merely parallel phenomena mirroring the reemergence in humans of what is essentially chimpanzee behavior? Are we just rats in a cage reverting to our worst type?

Whatever the answer, it is important for self-defenders, survivalists and martial arts instructors to realize that the threats against most of us are essentially that which the boy who scored that touchdown faced: to be attacked by a group, and pushed to the ground and kicked, because you have either accomplished something in life that they have not, or carry a valuable that they covet as a possession.

Why have I never seen a martial arts instructor, in the scores of schools and seminars I have attended, address the very real threat of being 'knocked over' by the crudest of means?

Even top NFL players find it difficult to remain on their feet when contact is made by a counterpart. Keep in mind that you, and your self-defense students, are going to be targeted by groups of larger and/or more athletic actors, who have banded together largely to limit their legal risks. Even if you or your student are killed all of the actors in a three-person or more group attack are very unlikely to face serious criminal charges. Social sanction for group violence is nearly universal in our society, while the individual who acts out against the group is universally vilified.

The answer to the question alluded to in the title of this article is that stomping and kicking a downed person is the equivalent of hiding in a crowd with the added benefit that the violent group has now grown in strength by accepting you among its members at the expense of that cohesion-building parody of humanity at your feet. You have arrived, have escaped alienation at the expense of one declared less worthy by the tribe that has just accepted you.

For you neo-conservatives and white-nationalists who are beginning to take up the banners of 'tribalism' and 'masculinity' in reaction to the deterioration of American society which you attribute to Latino and black culture, keep in mind that this is the form that tribalism takes in the modern world, the shoe to the downed skull; and that the implementation of this ethic as the 'jump-in' tool used by black and Latino gangs to develop cohesion was borrowed wholesale from white police departments and white [skinhead and biker] gangs.

Don't Get Boned

The only logical conclusion to the enforcement of tribal ethics in a postmodern society is an individual who lay helpless beneath the feet of a pack of apes wearing bloody shoes. I don't know why we are in such a hurry to devolve, because in Harm City, and on your local suburban gridiron, we are already there, devolving into apes intent on wiping out the remnant humans at our feet.

Stomping is a most understandable value in terms of culture building I suppose. So be a good citizen; watch football, practice your ground-and-pound, and support your local boot party.

Whacking Bad Guys

On Blunt Self-Defense Weapons

© 2013 James LaFond

For starters if you ever injure another human with a weapon you are in deep trouble. If it happens outside of your home, and not during the course of a clear case of self-defense, expect to go to jail and maybe prison.

If you are in a situation that you cannot survive without a weapon, than you can make three decisions that will minimize your legal liability:

1. Do not use a firearm!!

2. Do not use an edged weapon!

3. Use an unaltered blunt object as an improvised weapon.

What type of unaltered blunt weapons may you carry on your person?

1. This blunt object must not be a purpose built weapon and/or intended for police use: like a baton, an asp, a riot-stick, etc.

2. This blunt object must not have been altered to make it more damaging, lest it be defined as a sap or black jack.

3. You need to have a viable purpose other than self-defense [an act which few municipalities and states recognize as a right] for having this item at hand. This basically limits you to carrying light 'dog-walking' sticks, umbrellas, books, magazines; and perhaps a broken down pool cue stored in its carry case—but then only on nights when you go out shooting pool.

Examples of Justifiable Weapons at Hand

1. If you belong to a sports team, and the sport is in season, and you are going to and from practice or a game, than you may carry sporting objects that may be used as weapons. However, if you are a softball

player, you better be hauling a glove and ball as well as that nifty bat.

2. This same to and fro clause goes with martial arts equipment as well. Keep in mind though, that most martial arts weapons are illegal to carry in many localities, particularly blades and chucks.

3. If you want to carry a hammer you better be a carpenter and bring the belt as well. Bikers and truckers sometimes carry ball-peen hammers to check air pressure—or so they say.

The Best Unaltered Blunt Objects that May Be Used as Effective Defensive Weapons

1. A flashlight that takes D-cell batteries, the longer the better. Do remember to carry this item only at night. This is a favorite of police and security operatives.

2. A small umbrella gripped by the wire end, using the plastic handle as a striking end. These things only hold up for a few whacks, however you have a hard-edged striking surface mounted on a wire frame that provides a wiping action. This will easily scatter teeth across the street.

3. A cane or a walking stick specifically designed to aid walking, and not altered for striking.

4. A simple stick with no combat grip or lanyard. This is an item that is commonly used by people who walk dogs to keep dogs from getting at each other without getting bitten.

5. The rolled magazine. Held tightly in three thick rubber bands, this is just about as good as a small flashlight or umbrella.

Tactics

The less durable your weapon is, and the more dangerous your adversaries are, the more likely you are to have a need to strike the head. The head is the only debilitating stroke with a blunt object. The problem is it is the only kill stroke as well. For this reason you are always walking a knife-edge between legal liability and self-defense disaster. I prefer the less dangerous light stick and umbrella and even a rolled up magazine.

Stabbing the face is a good alternative to caving in the side of the head.

With the harder heavier weapons it will be difficult to strike the hands and knees and risky to get into the groin. The single most effective and underestimated stroke in stick-fighting is the vertical down stroke to the shoulder. This paralyses and even knocks out tough well-conditioned men that blow off dozens of the hardest stick strokes to the legs arms and torsos that you may imagine.

If it comes down to it, and you need to take a man out and he is open for a lateral stroke to the head, angle it down into his neck. This will slam into the same nerves that descend from the brain through the shoulders to the rest of the body.

With a lighter stick I recommend hand, elbow, face and knee shots.

Conclusion

As a practical matter it must be understood that those methods that favor the larger, stronger and more numerous party, such as grappling and blunt force, carry fewer government prohibitions and less severe penalties than those methods traditionally relied upon by smaller, weaker and less numerous parties, such as edged weapons and firearms.

Don't Get Boned

Many macho martial artists and gun enthusiasts invoke the old saying that 'it is better to be judged by twelve than carried by six.' In my view the saying could, in many cases, be amended to 'it is better to be beaten by six on the street than to be raped by twelve or shanked by two in prison.' I once spent three months of my life facing 'assault with a deadly weapon' and 'attempted murder' charges for defending my brother in my father's house. I got off, but those three months looking at 15 years amounted to the worst period of my life, and I was in my home. Had I been on the street those three months would have been the beginning of 15 years of hell.

Do yourself a favor and don't maim or kill an aggressor unless you have no reasonable alternative, especially if you are outside of your home.

Hacker John on Hood-rats

Harm City Handbook #4

© 2013 James LaFond

Last night I was on a scouting expedition to the local biracial bar to check up on the current crimescape. Five patrons from this bar have been attacked by packs of hood-rats and car loads of adult 'bankers' from July through early October.

At the bar I ran into Mary, a deli-clerk, who was being tutored on the fine art of urban survival by Hacker John. Thinking that my readers may be growing tired of my survival advice that always includes a large dose of long term legal sustainability advice at the expense of immediate lethal advice, I thought Hacker John might be well-received by a large segment of the Harm City readership. If you are a member of the 'better to be judged by 12 than carried by six' school of self-defense, you might want to nominate Hacker John as your spokesman.

Hacker John is an illegal cabbie, which places him on the fringes of the legal world. He will not be arrested for his activity unless he is operating at a 'cab stand' reserved for legit cabbies, or on a private lot whose owners do not sanction his activity, or if he charges fares. A 'hack' or 'gypsy cabbie' must take what is offered by the person they are giving a lift to. Their informal rules of operation follow the guidelines for the operation of 'sedans' [cabs without décor which are only supposed to pick up scheduled fares]. Their lot in life is often made more pleasant and lucrative when urban retail establishments agree to 'sanction' their activity through designating them 'courtesy drivers' and issuing a certificate.

Hacker John is an informal courtesy driver operating out of Fort Hoodrat under sanction of the minor league offensive lineman who provides security on the store front. He is a wiry, coal-faced man in his sixties who has exceeded the Harm City male life expectancy by two decades, and claims it is due to his 'no bullshit' worldview.

Without further ado...

"Now, if you alone and around this neighborhood, with all of these welfare mammas birthin' these hood-rats en lettin' them run wild, then you got to take precautions. Considerin' you female on foot it is the same as if you a male on your ass, sittin' in your sedan let's say."

"They come young, they come strong, swarmin' in packs. You've got to have that comeback capacity! It's a war out there: do or die, kill or be killed, eat or be ate."

"What you need is some good strong-sprayin' mace in the left hand and a ice-pick in the right! It is what's called for. You mace the face en stab! Mace, stab! Mace, stab! Mace, stab!"

"Oh so you think that extreme? Sheeeee, it a war out dare—Mace, stab! Mace, stab!"

I stand corrected. Oh, let us not pass over this stellar self-defense tutorial without a related word of caution. If you are grabbing a gypsy cab from Fort Hoodrat, or any other luxury retail outlet in Harm City, do not decline payment. I warned you.

Media Sponsored Terrorism & You

The 10 Dynamics of 'The Knockout Game' and How it Will Evolve at Your Expense

© 2014 James LaFond

Since November 2013 readers have been sending me links to videos and news reports about the so-called 'knockout game'. The causes for this brutal youth pastime are many and controversial. [See Stoning Baboons all the way down on the Harm City page]. I might deal with that on the Blog page. For now though, what does the existence of the 'knockout game' and the nature of the media response to it mean for you?

1. The fact that the media has gone along with the 'knockout game' semantics, and are referring to this form of criminal assault according to the self-serving label applied to it by the very perpetrators, and the fact that law enforcement personnel and legislators are continuing to use this wording, means that in case of civil or criminal prosecution

against a perpetrator or a defender, that the very terminology of the discussion will favor the player of the 'knockout game' as having been engaged in something juvenile rather than criminal. This has already happened. A local Maryland woman is facing legal action now for defending herself against a 'knockout game' group.

2. The players of the 'knockout game' have further insulated themselves from legal action by pursuing assault as a group activity, with only one 'hitter'. In the American judicial system accomplices to violent crimes other than murder are very rarely prosecuted. A recent light rail patron—a white woman who sounded entirely broken and terrified by her experience—who was attacked by a group of six [five serving as witnesses, encouragement, and lookouts], was horrified to find out that law enforcement released five without charges, as only the 'hitter' was 'involved'. This total ignorance of the group support dynamics of violence among law enforcement means that groups who initiate this violence will only be targeted for prosecution piecemeal, leaving the group itself innocent and at large to advance another hitter from its ranks against the next victim.

3. Virtually all perpetrators of 'knockout game' attacks are black youth, and virtually all victims are white adults. This has insured that the social dynamics of this phenomenon have and will remain obscured by liberal media filters.

4. Virtually all perpetrators are working class to middleclass black youth, not poor ghetto gangbangers, who have no time for such foolishness. This insures that their parents and local black community leaders will leap to their defense in case of any successful defense by a white adult targeted by them. The resulting legality deficit for the lone white adult defender is huge: the attacker is a youth and therefore a member of an unaccountable and protected segment of society; is furthermore a member of a protected racial minority; and is also the scion of upstanding community members who probably vote. For a white adult attacked today by a black youth group in this manner, the legal hazards of a successful physical defense approximate the hazards faced by a black man in the 1960s, who might have defended himself against a gang of middleclass white boys. This amounts to potentially deep legal shit.

5. The media versus Z-man on behalf of the martyred Skittle witch hunt of 2013 insured that

any lethal defense against a knockout game attack will effectively be faced with vast resources.

6. The primary reason why relatively affluent groups who wish to attack individuals generally select one hitter to take all of the risk is as a means of legal protection and also retaliation. If you defend yourself against a hitter he has 2 to 5 witnesses saying you attacked him or made a racial slur that justified his action. Never use lethal force against such an attack unless you want to be hanged by the news media.

7. 'Knockout game' players have further inoculated themselves from legal action by making certain that there is no accompanying property crime. This is likely to change, as these boys have unwittingly targeted Jews, and are therefore looking at a potential DOJ witch hunt of their own. New York politicians are already pushing for special penalties for the targeting of Jews, that will ironically—if this comes to pass—make a naked attempt to hurt someone more legally hazardous to the criminals than to hurt and rob them. If these civil rights based penalties make it into the legal code near you, then expect these middleclass kids looking to get their rocks off at your expense, to actually rob you as well, just so they can claim they were engaged in a

property crime and were not violating your civil rights.

8. The establishment of 'game' as part of the discourse on race-based and generation-based acts of gratuitous violence will insure lighter penalties for these crimes overall and heavily penalize any retaliation on the part of the target of such an attack. Now that it is widely established that a perpetrator of a 'knockout game' attack is supposed to accomplish his goal with only one strike, and cannot reasonably be expected to strike a second time, any counterpunch thrown by the defender will be legally seen as an act of revenge, not an act of defense.

9. 'Knockout game' players who are injured by a target of their crime will likely do what most people who attempt battery on a person who successfully defends themselves do; make a preemptive charge of battery against their intended victim, thus getting the crime reduced to a 'mutual combat' incident likely to be thrown out by a judge, or just settled with compensation to the party who was injured. Also, when this punk that tried to harmlessly knock you out, gets his nose bloodied and files a police report against you, the cop will give him your address!

10. The efforts of lawmakers to make the 'knockout game' a violation of civil rights, if successful, can likewise be expected to be turned on its head, with any black 'child' injured by a white adult while playing a media sponsored and legally and legislatively acknowledged 'game' invoking his civil rights, which will be claimed to have been violated.

Heads Up Bambi

I see the 'knockout game' as a cloaked black youth assault on a still majority white adult society, and in large measure a specific retaliation for Z-man's exoneration in the death of the sainted Skittle. I also see this as being as much about age as race. It is not at all class-based, except in those cases where robbery has been a component, and those, I believe, upon closer investigation, will have been found to involve the use of a weapon or multiple strikes. Youth versus adult property-based acts of violence are often class-based and just as commonly target blacks as whites [See Israel's account in When You're Food]. The targeting of whites is as much about limiting legal risks as anything, as the attackers now know themselves to be members of a protected class favored by the media.

Today's black suburban youth have been weaned on hate politics, and are now as soft and combat ineffective as their white counterparts. The 'knockout game' is an example of comfortably living children of limited privilege wanting to be as feared as their ghetto ancestors were. Not having the fortitude to engage in gang violence or survive prison, they may still make the dubious racial claim of the menacing black man that generations of southern white racist politicians and media bloodhounds bequeathed them as a self-limiting heritage, without risk to life, limb, or freedom. This is like white boys who won't play contact sports anymore pursuing video game violence to feel like a man for that fleeting moment.

Do note, that this 'game' originated with black ghetto youth journeying into white enclaves and public municipal spaces to have some brutal fun at the expense of more affluent members of a rival racial group. At that stage, this was largely payback for white police randomly jacking up black urban youth. They couldn't realistically beat up the cops. They could, however, make them look like lousy cops by beating up the people who the cops are supposed to be protecting.

I realize that the overall phenomena of increased black on white crime is much more nuanced than what I have addressed here in terms of the American media's agreement with our new class of violent black middleclass youth that hitting white adults and knocking them unconscious is just a 'game'. My main concern in the above article was to lay out the rationale, legal hazards for the defender, and likely evolution of, this latest wrinkle in our ongoing dystopian experiment.

I have been targeted for such incidents as this in the past and have avoided them through awareness and the silent communication that I would retaliate with lethal force. If you are like that poor woman that was interviewed about her attack on the light rail, to whom law enforcement responded by saying the light rail was safe because only one of the six youths that terrified her actually hit her, then do yourself a favor and stop fantasizing that there is some cop somewhere that cares if you are attacked and is willing to waste his time trying to prevent it. He is somewhere else, either banking traffic tickets for the county executive or battling urban drug gangs for the political puppets of an international bank.

Don't Get Boned

Modern American life is a watering hole and you need to wake up and smell your hunter Bambi. He's wearing name-brand body wash provided by his loving mother, who probably voted for the same presidential candidate that you did.

The Parking Lot

The Venerable Harm City Threat Zone

© 2014 James LaFond

The term 'street fighting' still drives me crazy. In the first place, fighting does not belong in a description of urban survival action, self-defense, or violent crime. And, even if one complies with the characterization of urban violence as 'fighting' who the hell does it in the street?

Really bro, you're going to 'whoop dat ass' in a river of steel, rubber, glass and fiberglass, rushing down on you like a toy truck plowing over little plastic army men?

I once did a study of 1,000 incidents of violence, 95% of which took place in Baltimore Maryland and surrounding counties. By checking the 'where' entry and adding them up, and dividing them by the big number, I discovered—not very much to my surprise—that a mere 17% of violence takes place on streets, and other road surfaces, such as highway off ramps, lanes, roads, boulevards, terraces, rural routes, interstate shoulders, private drive ways to long to fit in a Harm City block, oh yes, and avenues.

Of the 59% of action that senselessly occurred outside where witnesses, and even police, might view it, the 'kill box' if you will, was usually the 'access area' to a structure. Access ways such as stairs, sidewalks, and parking lots, generally offer the attacker concealment, mostly in the form of vehicles, and access to weapons, mostly stored within parked vehicles, as well as quick egress, in the form of that self-same chariot of suburban access. If I could give my Harm City readers one piece of survival advice, it would be to go to red alert when on parking lots. Parking lots are ideal for abductions. Vehicles stopping and starting in traffic to grab someone are much more noticeable than vehicles doing the same on a parking lot.

Below are three brief anecdotes concerning recent Harm City parking lot encounters or threats.

Miss Sandy was running the register at Fort Hood-rat when an elderly lady attempted to pay for groceries with an expired WIC voucher. The lady—

in her 70s—then said, "Oh you white ghetto bitch. I ought ta go ta ma car en ged my gun en shoot yo ass! Watch you back bitch!"

George, a 'return clerk' on the Cheap Guys R Us night crew, was racking up carts outside after the midnight close, when a homeless man approached him, demanding access to the store. George's pleas that he did not have the keys, and that the store was closed only brought threats from the homeless man. George managed to evade the man and bang on the windows enough to summon the night crew. After his rescue by the night captain, George is now brought in at 11:30 so that he does not have to field the constant threats from people who want access to a closed store. This is incredibly common. On two different occasions I had cops threaten me for not opening a closed food market for their shopping needs. I dealt with well over a thousand threats from drunks and weirdos who, as a store manager, I had denied access to a closed store.

Last year a friend who is a combat arts instructor was attacked by two men on a parking lot, over a parking space. He KO'd them both. I cannot give any details as this is still in litigation. When the case is closed I will get a full interview. I can tell you this. As the men had parked their car so as to block him in his space while they attacked, he moved it so that he could leave, making sure not to run over any bodies or damage any vehicles. Shortly thereafter he was arrested for grand theft auto for moving the car used by his attackers to trap him!

The surface on which you defend yourself will mostly likely be paved with asphalt or concrete, but it probably won't be a street.

Colby en Crew

Dognapping Countermeasures

© 2014 James LaFond

On Januray 21 I wrote a piece on the dozen or so missing dogs in my neighborhood. These dogs were lost, ran away, were eaten by foxes, or were dognapped from fall 2012 through the end of 2013. Most of these were small lap dogs that probably fell prey to the very large fox and his two friends who prowl this neighborhood, having been driven into the city by the booming coyote population in Harford County. Two of these dogs—the larger ones—were definitely abducted by human predators.

Over the past four days I have seen five new 'missing dog' or 'stolen dog' signs in a one mile long, quarter mile wide swath of Northeast Baltimore that I covered. And I did not cover it all, only 40%. Some of the light poles in my area are literally layered with missing dog signs. Bringing a dog into this neighborhood is about as pet-friendly as sending your sixteen year old daughter to peddle girl scout cookies at the local crack-house would be child friendly.

A Staffordshire terrier named Colby leaped his fence and has not been seen.

The other four dogs were abducted: a young shepherd mix, a young husky type, a mid-sized young hound/shepherd mix; and a bulldog. These dogs are all too large for the large fox to haul over a three foot fence. One was seen being taken by young men. It is obvious that professional dognappers have wrangled area pets for pit-bull bait.

Dog fighting in Baltimore is accepted by most of the population and most law officers. In the mid 1990s the premier dog fighting venue was on Asquith, in the driveway of a chop shop, a stone's throw [even if your mother was throwing the stone] from the Northeastern District Courthouse. By day the place was swarming with cops, lawyers and judges, and overrun by gangbangers, hoodlums, dealers, pimps, hos, Jons, and dog fighting fans by night.

Don't Get Boned

The boys, youths and men who abduct these dogs have dog wrangling skills and equipment. The dogs are sold to dog fighters, who feed these household pets to their brutalized prize-fighting dogs—your coddled pet fed alive to a born and raised killer. This would be like dragging a middle aged accountant out from behind a desk and throwing him in a cage with Phil Baroni to fight for his life.

I realize that most dog owners would rather have their car stolen than their dog. What with the poor quality of humans out there, the family dog is usually more agreeable company than what is staggering through my neighborhood on two feet on any given hour.

I have notice a trend that once identified, can be used as the foundation for foiling these creeps. The portion of Northeast Baltimore I live in was once an orchard, surrounded by the estates of the well-to-do. There are dozens of dilapidated mansions within a quarter mile from the large rundown frame house where I rent a room. Once you get back in the neighborhoods off of the secondary streets you see a mix of post WWII residential housing with small obscured fenced in yards, and pre WWII fat cat digs with vast fenced in back, front and side yards. The more compressed backyards of the most recent housing offer fewer dognapping opportunities. The estate like remains of farm houses and mansions put the fenced in pet at risk. These kinds of plush shaded yards are paradise for a dog and its doting owner, but...

These yards are scouted via vehicle. Dogs are generally only stolen on foot in row house neighborhoods via alleys. If you have a large fenced yard for your dog, do not let him or her out for extended periods. If it is a small dog be particularly mindful to accompany your pet into the yard at night to warn off fox attacks. If you have any size dog do not let it stay outside unattended for lengthy or predictable periods. If you let the dog out for one hour every day after work while you get your shower—it will get snagged and fed to the canine version of 20-year-old Mike Tyson.

6 by 2 city blocks

4 days

4 stolen dogs

I of course would like to sentence dognappers to be thrown in the cage with an MMA fighter. Realistically, I think the public would be better served—providing we were living in the phony construct we imagine wherein the police are assigned to protect and serve—if police K-9 units would be used to target dognapping and dofighting operations.

Those cops would give a shit.

That Handle on Your Back

Required Reading for Load-bearing Urban Human Prey

© 2014 James LaFond

Are you a student, a pedestrian, a gaming geek, or any other type of prey species that hauls your immediately accessible goods in a backpack?

Backpacks may be used as weapons, when loaded with books; a heavy flail that is only good for smashing a downed person. This is typically how a backpack is used against its owner after the backpack itself has been used as a handle to toss the owner to the ground. Below are some tips on urban backpack usage that will help minimize your kinetic liability.

1. Make sure the shoulder straps on your backpack are as loose as possible so that you can easily slip one shoulder out.

2. Practice taking off your backpack with one hand by sliding it under the shoulder strap at your hip and turning out of it, letting the pack hang from the crook of the other arm, where it might be retained or used.

3. Never buckle the waist or chest strap unless you are walking a good distance and have a potential weapon [like an umbrella or rolled up magazine] in your hand. In such cases a small hand weapon like a pen should also be in easy reach.

4. When walking mid distances just sling one strap over your left shoulder. This will help protect you against stabs, almost all of which come at a low rising angle to the left side, and leave your right hand free to fight. The most important aspect of this carry posture is that you cannot be grabbed by the pack and thrown down.

5. In close quarters, as when boarding and offloading, carry your pack in your left hand by the top strap, so it will be instantly at hand to use as a flail, shield, or blinder. People are commonly attacked when offloading from mass transit, when accessing and leaving vehicles, and when using access ways to buildings.

6. When your ass exceeds the value of your pack, and you are in a freestanding situation, place it at your feet. An aggressor that attempts to grapple you risks tripping on it, and he will not be able to effectively punch you without stepping around it. With both of your hands free, use it as tactical obstruction. If he bends to pick it up, kick his teeth into the gutter with those steel-toed boots you should be wearing.

Taking The Eyes

Notes on Training For a Blinding Defense

© 2014 James LaFond

I have had some female self-defense enthusiasts and a few smaller men ask me how to best prepare to defend against big, powerful men.

I always say, "Take the eyes."

Legally, you do not want to eye gouge, or do some fantasy kung fu eye-removal technique, as you can face up to 20 additional years on a maiming charge.

I am talking about finger jabbing or spearing.

Ancient Egyptian and Greek boxers did it.

I have done it.

You can do it.

Don't Get Boned

The first step is to develop a good fist jab under a boxing coach

The second step is finger conditioning. Never finger jab at full finger extension, but with the fingers slightly coned with the longer middle finger stacked up in the middle. Be mindful to curl the pinkie and thumb slightly under the ring finger and pointing finger.

Make this finger cone or spear and shadow box.

Practice sliding your finger spear out from a fist and retracting the speared fingers back into a fist as you shadow box.

Target the eyes, not the throat. If the eyes are not open, target the chin with the fist. Don't try to spear through hands.

If you watch MMA you will notice that many fights feature accidental eye pokes. These are accidents. Imagine if they tried to do this? Sparring with open finger gloves has taught me that eyes are easier targets than one would suppose as fingers [unlike fists] are actually funneled into the eye by the sunken nature of the socket. Glide in over the cheek, slide up beside the nose, or go right in.

Don't Get Boned

You must be able to withstand spearing the forehead of a hard head, because that is what will happen two out of three times. Fill a bucket with rice or dried beans and practice pushing your finger spear into it. Also practice with fingers spaced at various widths.

Hang a piece of paper with a face drawn on it from a door jam or from a speed bag platform and practice jabbing the eyes while moving. You want to keep your fingernails trimmed to prevent splintering them, unless you're into the whole Dracula thing. You want to practice flicking the eye and spearing it, the later being digitally and legally more risky. You want to be able to pop that paper and punch holes in it.

After your fingers are conditioned practice finger jabbing the speed bag and or the double-ended bag. Don't do this with the reflex bag or heavy bag.

Eventually, move up to finger jabbing the focus patch on the focus mitts.

Finger jab sparring can be done asymmetrically, with the finger jabber wearing work gloves with suede tips and head gear. The other partner wears boxing gloves and goggles. The defense against the finger jab—and the straight spear hand with the rear hand—is to intercept the finger spear with a punch. This will cause a nice crunching sound if done properly.

Your weapons are:

1. The flicking finger jab

2. The spearing finger jab

3. The straight rear hand finger spear

4. The palm up finger spear with either hand. Do not arc this like an uppercut

5. The thumb rake in the clinch

6. The palm up finger dig to an aggressor grappling low with their head down

Don't rip the eye out. Just scratch up the cornea to cause them to desist. If they are coked-up or methed-up then spear the eye to shock the brain.

Do not neglect the fist as you may injure your fingers and need to ball them up, or might be dealing with an open chin and closed highline. Feinting to the body with the fist and then shooting a raking spear hand across the cheek can be very effective.

Wimps, Hotheads & Head-cases

A Checklist for Breaking Minds: An Excerpt From
the Upcoming Book Taboo You

© 2014 James LaFond

Keeping in mind the fear trajectory discussed above
under the King and Queen of Emotions, below is a
menu of vulnerability cues to consider where
adversaries are concerned. As any boxing coach will
tell you this is the area where the fight takes place,
in the minds of the fighters. With the exception of
remarkably gifted fighters such as Ali, and
masterful talents like Mayweather, fighters who do
not bring the following characteristics under
control through discipline, don't go far.

As far as survival situations in urban environments
go, it is the psychological discipline cultivated by
the trained fighter that accounts for his success far
more often than his sport specific body mechanics. I
must say, of the hundreds of fighters I have faced in
bouts and duels, I have only 'broken' a few of them

over hundreds of victories. Where the hundreds of criminals, workplace bullies, abusive supervisors, and even packs of feral dogs that have threatened me in everyday life are concerned, I've broken the will of nearly all of them.

The process is simple:

1. Do not back down

2. Do not give attack cues [like calling a black man the n-word]

3. Utilize their emotive cues as a veritable control panel for their psyche

A glance at this list and an assessment of people you know, will reveal the fact that virtually every person you come into day-to-day contact with is at or beyond the psychological breaking point, and hence easily manipulated or broken. The following cues indicate emotional vulnerability in that the observation of these behaviors is sure proof that this person cannot consistently control them. Keep in mind that there are many gradations of vulnerability within each cue.

Emotive Cue Checklist

Don't Get Boned

1. Fearful

2. Angry [the surest indication of a brittle and easily broken mind]

3. Talkative

4. Argumentative

5. Loud

6. Boastful

7. Pitiful [crying and whining]

8. Seeks approval

9. Needs approval

10. Impressed by size, appearance and style

Fearfulness [#1] and the need for approval [#9] are responsible for the low level of participation and retention of women in combat sports. Coaching most women is a constant exercise in the infusion of will into a soul that is not content to be alone under stress. Coaching female fighters is exhausting due to the almost sure presence of both of these factors. Imagine three, four, or six cues in one person?

The duality that causes most male combat athletes to wash out early is a combination of anger [#2] with the tendency to be impressed by size and other appearance issues [#10]. Fighters that cannot conquer their anger—which is a manifestation of their inner weakness—do not progress normally, and are essentially retarded in terms of combat preparation.

Harm City High

The 'Violence Guy' Takes A Look at 'Racial Tensions' in Harm City

© 2014 James LaFond

'Digital Harbor' is a technology magnet high school in South Baltimore, my old stomping ground from 1996-2006. Recently the front page of the Baltimore Sun has been whining about 'racial tensions' at this school.

There was a classroom disagreement between an Hispanic youth and a black youth which resulted in a planned fight after school—after the old tradition—which resulted in a hospital visit of the heroic, and no doubt vastly outgunned, Latino kid. Social media threats from black students ensued. Adults put the news of this together with recent robberies and assaults on Latinos by blacks and by this week most Latino students were staying home from Digital Harbor. The Sun Paper, is reporting the story as if blacks and Hispanics are at each other's throats, when, in fact, Hispanics are cowering in fear from the blacks, who vastly out number, outweigh, and outgun them.

Disclaimer

I am a Darwinist who does not belief in solutions, so I see no point in going into the 'whys' behind the facts I shall detail below. However, I have many do-gooding friends who look to me for answers to violence. Again, I do not believe violence can be eliminated, or even significantly curbed, and will take issue with those who say that Man is less violent than he was. All I am offering here is a 'battle-space assessment' in case your Mary Poppins balloon sets down in Harm City and you find your tender self in the proximity of our feral teenagers.

The Crimescape

Out here, at the LaFond Plantation, where my wenches, whelps and bucks labor in the basement and backyard so that I might live the high life and wax philosophic online, I have been asked, by my faithful overseer, about my opinion concerning the recent 'racial tensions' in the most thoroughly re-gentrified white enclave in Harm City. The humorous aspect of this is that 98% of South Baltimore residents are white, work in teenage-proof corporate towers, send their children to gated private schools, and are completely unaffected by the spectacle of 200 pound black teens working over 100 pound Latino teens in the gutter as they enjoy their microbrew and entrée at the local hipster café. South Baltimore children do not attend Digital Harbor. Almost all students are bussed in.

In 1996, when I was sent to South Baltimore to merchandize frozen foods for Boss Bob at Upscale Eats for Soft White Teats, I encountered an 80% yuppie homesteader population and a 20% stay-behind urban white trash population descended from CSX Railway employees who migrated from West Virginia from 1920 through 1960. When Cuz and Bro had moved into South Baltimore in the mid 1980s it was 50/50. This was ideal for those yuppie urban homesteaders, as there were plentiful white trash babes to take home, violate, and evict in the morning—more than willing as they were to carry the genes of an educated white man with a good income, and like their brothers not too difficult to outwit. In the meantime, as you bedded their sister, these urban Neanderthals like Duncan, Crazy Steve, Lille Berry, and Ricky Mason [see When You're Food, my five-time not nominated Nobel entry] were kicking the oppressed shit out of any blacks who attempted to violate their Forbidden Zone.

Now the white trash is gone! Extinct!!

Who will hold the line against the home boys?

No one.

In the late 1990s two of my female cousins lived in South Baltimore. One dated a black dude and was mugged—brutally on one occasion in front of witnesses—three times by black youth gangs. She asked me not to write that they were black as she did not want me to reinforce the stereotype of the black male criminal. My other female cousin was married to a pussy who moved her and the kids out to the county after he complained to me about black Digital Harbor students threatening him and pissing on his front steps.

Rather than complain, the current South Baltimore yuppies should be happy that the black kids who are bussed in from the drug crime enclaves of Cherry Hill and West Baltimore on the #64 and #1 buses have been provided with smaller and less numerous human prey in the form of the children of Hispanic immigrants with no criminal background. This frees the wife up for shopping as opposed to being robbed as soon as she walks out front.

Although the Sun Paper, Mouthpiece of the People's Republic of Maryland, states that there is 'built-up tension between Latinos and African-Americans' [a term that no black in Baltimore outside of the political, academic or news establishment uses] in Baltimore, the photos in their stories prove this a lie.

Only Latinos group together for protection.

Only Latinos hold hands and pray for peace.

Baltimore is a hunting matrix. Digital Harbor is a watering hole where cubs practice low level predation, and the Latino students are the baby gazelle they practice on. The Sun Paper misleadingly labels Black-on-Latino attacks as 'fights'.

The cops say that the attacks are not racially motivated. They have to say this to appease the tourist conscious Mayor's Office. I, however, agree with their political line on factual grounds. These attacks are not racially motivated. As I am not currently tracking violence through interviews and observations in South Baltimore, but in North, Northeast, and East Baltimore, I will take you through the identical behaviors in these areas, plagued with far more frequent violence that has not achieved any notoriety because of the lack of news paper selling hate politics, and the absence of an affluent backdrop.

'My Nigga Went Ta War!'

Thus spake the leader of a high school gang set this morning, at 7:23 as I sat two feet from him. I was on my way home. He was on his way to school. We were on the #55 bus from Eastern Baltimore County headed to Northern Baltimore County through Northeast Baltimore City. He and his friends had transferred out from East Baltimore to the Northeast Baltimore school where they would do battle in the cafeteria, and in the halls, and in the restrooms, and everywhere but where the City Cop is on the front sidewalk.

Don't Get Boned

Their enemies were 'light skinned boys' from West Baltimore. These guys were dark skinned, about 75% African and 25% European. However, since all people with more than one eighteenth sub-Saharan African blood in their veins are considered 100% African-American in this depraved nation, this is not 'racial'. It is also not newsworthy as all injured parties are black males who no one really cares about [unless they are attacked by white males], and all of the aggressors are black males—who may not be profiled as aggressors in New News America without the profiler suffering charges of racism.

The interesting thing about the conversation between the three black youths was that they did not boast, they did not high-five or fist-bump. They did not congratulate each other on their performance in yesterday's fight. No, the conversation was purely centered on technique: should you 'sneak up and punch to the eye?'; should you 'sneak up and slam'; should you 'face off en crack dat niga to da flo?' In short, what is the most effective method for attacking the enemy so that the rest of the 'crew' will be able to 'do damage' before the lone City Cop gets on the scene.

Obviously these guys will turn their attentions to Latinos if they are available for they are more readably distinguishable as enemies, less numerous, and small. However, since none of these guys know what a Latino is [I hear them argue about Latino racial status all the time, and it is a hoot.], I doubt if such attacks will be motivated by racial hatred. In fact, I bet my left nut that every one of these black boys would line up to kiss Jennifer Lopez on the cheek—well, maybe not the cheek you would kiss...

The Current Harm City Violence Facts

Over the past year I have interviewed people concerning, or have witnessed, 42 acts of violence. This area of Baltimore is roughly 55% black and 40% white, with Latinos, Middle Easterners, and Asians comprising the balance of 5%. Here is how they break down.

1. Of 42 violent incidents, 5 were fights, 1 involving a white and black male youth, and 4 involving black women fighting each other.

2. Of 42 acts of violence 37 were unprovoked attacks.

3. Of 37 unprovoked attacks three were committed by white police officers against 1 white man and 2 black youths.

4. Of the 34 unprovoked attacks by citizens who were not law officers, all were committed by blacks.

5. Of the 34 unprovoked attacks by blacks 3 were committed by black women.

6. Of the 34 unprovoked attacks by blacks 4 involved a white accomplice, which negates any racial motivation.

7. Of the 34 unprovoked attacks by blacks 3 targeted Latinos.

8. Of the 34 unprovoked attacks by blacks 17 targeted white persons, all of whom were low income people.

9. Of the 34 unprovoked attacks by blacks 14 targeted blacks.

10. Of the 14 blacks that were attacked by other blacks, 1 was a female.

Making sense of these small numbers is beyond me. However the only trend I see is that virtually all violence in my third of Baltimore is committed by Blacks, with the remainder committed by white cops. I know for a fact that West Baltimore is even more skewed to black perpetrators and black targets. So, my guess is, if you manage to protect the Latino kids at Digital Harbor, the light-skinned black kids and whatever poor white kid [who will never make it into a police report or news story because he is poor and white] remains, will become the new 'enemy', and be summarily attacked.

Folks, this is nothing more complicated than the results of declaring war on drugs, tradition, and God, thinking that Nancy 'Just-Say-No' Regan and Hillary Goddamned Clinton would invent better methods to socialize children than the 10,000 year old traditions we scrapped along the way to Harm City High.

Don't Get Boned

'Standing Off'

Notes on Vigilance

© 2014 James LaFond

JoJo is a local lady who has taken the bus with me on occasion. Recently, with the spate of attacks on women by male youths, she requested that I occasionally stop by the bus stop she uses in my neighborhood. She gave me the times of her work commutes. She reasoned that If she was seen even occasionally with such a disreputable Urban Neanderthal as myself, that any hoodlums who might be tempted to plan her demise might think again.

The other day I skulked on up to her first stop on the way home. She had purchased a sports drink and peanuts for me so I felt compelled to break out the bus ticket and see her all the way home, across all three stops. She is an older lady who can't manage the two mile walk across town, so spends over an hour in an L-shaped commute: two short walks, two waiting periods, and two short bus sides.

At the first stop I stood and she sat.

At the second stop, in a high-crime locale where thugs have shot it out with cops, I sat down next to her and another lady, an elderly widow, who sat next to a woman and her two children. Then a group of five teen age boys began swaggering in our direction. They did not appear to be genuine criminals, just wannabe tough guys.

When they reached bum-rush range I stood and walked over toward the light pole by the curb, so I had something to put my back to that I could not be pinned against. I then began planning my attack. I decided to sink a right to the body of the tall kid and spear the eyes of the muscle guy, then imagined various target-of-opportunity scenarios. I was not considering self-defense. I don't believe in self-defense. I was simply mulling over my attack options; options which were not put into effect, as the youths did not trouble JoJo.

The boys were then joined by two others, discussed 'banking some niggas down da way', and were off about their violent business. After the bus picked us up JoJo said, "I noticed you stood up when those boys came by. Was that because you thought they were up to no good?"

"I never sit in the presence of an able-bodied male who I do not trust—ever; unless it is on the bus, which does not count as sitting because you can use the bus' energy to launch an attack from a seated position if you time the banking, acceleration, and braking."

"You made me nervous at first, when you stood and started to pace. But then they gathered away from the bench instead of strutting around like they usually do, and I felt safe. I had such a nice time talking with Mrs. Gans. She just lost her husband and still has such a good spirit."

We were soon offloading at a drug-corner. The thug standing there sized me up and I returned the favor with a truce nod, which he confirmed with his own. This is a common body sign used by blacks in Baltimore that says, 'We're enemies, but not now.' It is typically used by criminals as a sign of temporary respect when they are with their female non-combatants or attending church or funeral services, or when the ultimate enemy—the cops—are about in force. A truce nod does not mean 'I am tougher than you' or 'I want to be your friend', both of which signals will get you in deep in a hurry.

I walked JoJo back into her neighborhood past one crack den and a vacant. The rest of the area was pretty nice away from the main road. She asked me to sit out on the steps with her for a while with the following explanation, concerning her roommate's children, "You see that pasty white faggot in that minivan, pulling through the four-way?"

I dead-locked the fat man in the eyes as he cruised by.

"That pervert, and three other white perverts, cruise this neighborhood looking for kids to molest right about now when school starts to let out. That's why I sit out here and give those fuckers the eye. I probably can't handle those punks on the bus stop. But I have a butcher knife by the door. If any of these perverts stops to talk to a kid around here his head is getting pinned to the dashboard."

I finished my drink and said, "Well, it looks like you've got this situation under control. I need to start hoofing it home."

Don't Get Boned

This is the kind of self-policing that men in traditional cultures and in low income areas have typically done. It has largely eroded in suburban America, no matter the ethnicity of the residents. The violence of our blooming narcostate should usher in its return. It won't happen though, until women like JoJo speak up and call the men in their lives down off of the degendered fence they have been shunted off to.

When Your Back is To The Wall

The Best Home Defense Knife

© 2014 James LaFond

I have taken a lot of heat from knife gurus, knife manufacturers, and knife enthusiasts from recommending that one not use a knife for street defense. Look, I am—as far as I know—the most experienced live steel knife fighter on the planet.

I wrote The Logic of Steel, the King James version of 'getting stabbed' bibles.

I like to stab people, and have done so in duels and in criminal altercations.

I have ripped people apart with blades, sharp and dull, and did not feel a bit of remorse.

I like knives, have been sleeping with a three pound bowie knife for 35 years. My most durable human sleeping companion only lasted 15 years, and when she told me the knife had to go, I moved into a separate room.

I love blades!

And I am telling you, don't carry a blade for defense unless you are willing to do time in a joint where they cross swords of a non-metallic kind.

But, if you are looking for a reliable home defense tool, that will not go through the wall and kill your neighbor, does not have to be registered with our Master, and can be bought by the case load so that there is one in every corner of every room [actually, in my bathtub, I keep a scuba knife, as it won't rust.], I am suggesting a knife.

What kind of knife?

The brands change, but they are available in dollar stores and grocery stores in the dollar section for $1 apiece.

"One dolla!"

Yes one American dollar for one Chinese knife that is sharper than anything our hairy ancestors were hacking each other up with in the Black Forest while the Chinese were experimenting with paper currency and chemical weapons.

This is a Chinese made butcher knife with a full tang handle, retainable grip, and a 9 inch blade— the shining porn star of kitchen cutlery.

The Bowie knife is a redesign of the ages old butcher knife. When that big goon Jim Bowie decided that the best way to win a sword fight was to grab the little twerp that just ran you through and shove mom's butcher knife into his belly and twist it until he 'heard his heartstrings sing', he didn't have to do much redesign work.

Everyone has a butcher knife at home, so there is an excuse for it to be there and at hand. When they come for you in your home, send their hand across the floor. Remember to compassionately call the ambulance before the police, give the fool a clean towel, and use your salad tongs to put the hand into a zip-lock bag.

Oh yeah, and thank the Chinese.

On Getting Stabbed

Backstabbing Survivor Makes What He Thinks May
Be His Last Phone Call

© 2014 James LaFond

If you are a survivalist, knife enthusiast, or self-
defense practitioner, check out the link below. Be
sure and listen to the radio interview of the food
truck operator that saw this two-on-one revenge
attack that carried over from a previous day's
altercation.

http://newyork.cbslocal.com/2014/06/24/stabbin
g-victim-walks-into-queens-mcdonalds-with-knife-
in-his-back/

In the photo you can plainly see a fixed blade knife,
said to be a kitchen knife [I told you so], sticking out
of this man's back. It is an obvious case of an ice-
pick stab, and a calculated one at that. Rage-based
ice pick stabs to the back usually rain down on the

shoulder blades. This sucker was pumped in with an aimed hammering motion.

Hopefully the man survived. He benefitted from some quick thinking bystanders. Dom, who sent this to me, said he's been into this burger joint countless times.

With the ruling feminist oligarchy ever encroaching on citizens' freedom to carry firearms for personal defense, and the bountiful supply of cheap knives, I expect a rise in stabbings nationwide, particularly in cities with strict gun laws. It is ever less likely that a knifer has to worry about being that walking punch line that brought a knife to a gunfight.

If this happens to you or anyone you care about, first count yourself lucky that the stabber left the knife in to plug that whole he just made, and second, do not remove it! The best thing that could happen to you if you get stabbed, particularly around the lungs, is that the knife stays in.

'Look Son!'

A Man Question by From Brooklyn Shane

© 2014 James LaFond

I am not exactly a CNN bureau chief, but JamesLaFond.com has become something of a news clearing house for street violence reports. Below is a report and a link from Shane, one of my East Coast reporters:

Brooklyn Shane's Heads Up

"Look Son!"

"Your Mayor is a stupid bitch..but then again so is mine.."

http://washington.cbslocal.com/2014/06/25/balti more-city-mayor-speaks-out-against-knockout-game/

Don't Get Boned

Okay, knowing Shane as I do, having gotten drunk with him on occasion, I can tell you that the above statement is in fact a challenge to my off-bruised intellectual mass to make sage sense of whatever my mayor of questionable intellect has to say in the above link. I have pasted the text from the story below. If you click on the link you will also be treated to a brief audio report.

The News Story

LANHAM, Md. (WNEW) – After two recent "knockout games" left several people in Baltimore injured, the city's mayor has decided to speak out.

WNEW Annapolis Bureau Chief Karen Adams reports that Baltimore City Mayor Stephanie Rawlings-Blake is disgusted by the attacks and says they are not a game.

"They don't understand the consequences," Rawlings-Blake said. "If you knock someone out, you could think its a joke and you'll hurt somebody – that person could die. And then your life is ruined for some stupidity that you and your friends think is fun. It's just not worth it."

Rawlings-Blake said Wednesday that adults in the city can help to prevent these crimes by being more involved in the lives of children who may be roaming the streets.

This comes days after two incidents that police believe are connected to the knockout game, which involves a group of people trying to knock someone out with a single punch.

This past weekend, a Texas man in town for his college orientation was reportedly punched in the head outside the Baltimore Harbor Hotel by a group of youths. Last week, two brothers claimed they chased down a group of about 20 kids after being punched. Police say a 16-year-old boy was later arrested.

However, the violence is not exclusive to Baltimore.

In November, a woman in Northwest Washington told police she was attacked by a group of eight people, with one hitting her in the head.

The "games" have caused deaths in New York, New Jersey and Missouri.

Sage Commentary

Mayor O'Mamma is guilty of a blatantly amoral appeal to the soulless youth she intends as her audience. She has not made a stupid statement in this instance. You see Shane, there is no other way to appeal to Harm City youth than to appeal to their sense of inconvenience, and this may only be done via their sense of innocence.

Yes, all hip-hop identified youth are innocent, the very neo-Rousseauian paragons of primordial nobility. Seriously, anytime you address a Harm City youth as a perpetrator or suspect, they stop listening and start lying and denying. She knows that they intend to hurt people. The older associates of these kids have already whacked one of her family members. To have a chance they will hear anything, you must preface your statement with assurances that they are innocent. This stems from the criminal versus cop culture that is the cornerstone of Harm City dynamics. Always deny, then lie. It's liked these kids were all raised by Bill Clinton.

Permit me to translate her entire statement, as if she had spoken in private to a group of these fine youngsters:

"We know you're just follin'. But, these crackers have soft heads—it's not like dropping the phone book on Uncle Rodney's head while he's sleeping off that forty buzz—and one of them could split open, and if they die, you'll have to decide which one of your set is going to do the time. And then you won't be able to hang out with that person until they get out of Juvy in three years. Now, unless you are the ho giving head, or the dude with the dope connect, you could very well have your friends snitch you out, and then it's your ass—your dumbass doing three years in Juvy. That's what I'm talkin' about."

Being a politician who lives and dies by crime stats, and not always certain if she can trust the police to 'juke' the stats to her advantage, she wants this to go away, sees it as a 'game' as 'stupidity', because that is how it is reported, and she is a creature of the media. She buys into their template as part of her function. The problem with her reasoning is the same as every other political figurehead's reasoning; it is shortsighted. She, like most of law enforcement, and all of the media, does not give these kids enough credit, does not know where this knockout game is going.

The knockout game is a gang building activity, an external 'jump-in', with some stranger getting blooded instead of the wannabe gangbanger. In that sense it is am evolutionary improvement on the jump-in—Darwin would approve.

More ominously, this is practice. The knockout game, as played, is precisely how blind-side muggers attack victims. The only difference is that the 'game players' run away instead of stomping and robbing the target of the attack, which makes this much less risky legally than an actual mugging. As the Mayor's statement implies, criminals and aspiring criminal youth will try to avoid doing time. When these kids grow up, they will cruise in cars 'five deep' with four leaping out and 'running up on somebody' who will be hit from behind or the side, usually with a right to the right side of the head, and hopefully knocked to the pavement where they can be stomped. Ghetto youth understand this type of preparation. Many of them train their pet pit bulls on small domestic 'bait dogs' that are grabbed from yards.

Thanks for the heads up Son!

Anthony's Scooter

Stopping a Property Crime in Progress

© 2014 James LaFond

1:30 a,m,, Wednesday, 7/9/14

Anthony, a small adult man, who works the graveyard shift and resides in Baltimore County, was unwinding on his night off, enjoying a night 'away from the grind'. Anthony is a low income guy who owns a new motor scooter which he rides to work, and to play on the pool league he competes in. Anthony looks a lot like comedian Bob Newhart did in the 1970s.

"My neighbor comes home, knocks on my door, and says that kids are messing with my scooter. I go look outside and there are these four punks—fourteen, fifteen I'd say—pushing, and pulling and tugging at my scooter. I keep it chained to the pole in the lot out back. They don't have bolt cutters so they're trying to use the scooter as a lever to break the chain—and the mirror, the plastic body, is all getting busted up.

"I ran to the phone and got nine-one-one. The dispatcher said they were five minutes out. I said that in five minutes there would be nothing left of my scooter and that I was going to run them off. The dispatcher told me not to go outside, to let the 'responding officer' handle it.

"I hung up, got my bat, and ran outside. The three smart ones ran off into the woods behind Pulaski Highway. The dummy ran up the alley so I lit out after him. By the time I ran him to the end of the alley a cop pulled up—really it was like four minutes—and took him down.

"He gave me a verbal warning for having the bat and taking things into my own hands. Said there was a better way. He said it was a bad idea, that they could have gotten all of them if I had waited. Two other cops showed up too. He told the kid that he was either ratting out his friends or taking it all himself. He gave me a call back number so I could call in the estimate from the bike shop.

"A friend told me I should not have called, should just have gone out there and cracked some heads.

You write about this violence stuff. Do you think that would have been the right thing to do? Could I have gotten away with it?"

"Well, I've read the Annotated Code of Maryland a few times and its real murky on lot of stuff. It is clear on the fact that you can only use force to protect yourself or others from harm, and then only just enough force, and only when you have no other reasonable option. Nowhere is there a provision for avenging damage to you property, or even using force to protect your property. Also, keep in mind that you would never lay that bat on all four dudes, probably not even two. So then you have two or three witnesses telling the cops that you snuck up on their buddy and clocked him. Hospitals charge more for repairing humans than bike shops do for repairing scooters. Even if it just went civil, which is unlikely, you would have come up short there too."

"Yeah, that's pretty much what the cop said, that violence should not be the first answer. But it just gets to you after a while that you have to take all of this shit from people. The cops were on it—did their job last night."

I am currently reading opinions by the Maryland Court of Special Appeals, as the code itself is obviously a rough guide for legal arguments, not a precise set of behavioral rules like we have in sports or table top war gaming. I'll be doing a piece on this before summer is out.

A Skulker in the Yard

Dealing With the Nosey Lone Male

© 2014 James LaFond

At 12:30 this afternoon I was 11 pages from completing my proof of Planet Buzzkill; in writing mode, not wanting to be interrupted by the help here on the plantation. As luck would have it a security concern arose while my overseer was away on some errand—it is just so tediously impossible to keep track of these people!

My overseer's wench burst through the door to my study and blurted, "Sorry. There is a guy in the yard, a guy in the yard. He's walking next door, he's circling the house. He was just on the side—he's black! I'm freaked out. I need you to do something."

I stood up, ready to spring into action, and something felt kind of strange below the waist. We looked down and I said, "How about I start with pants."

Don't Get Boned

Look, I'm a well-to-do writer and am permitted my eccentricities, and I assure you, that I have a pair of shorts on as I write this.

I hopped into my shorts, and realizing that this was probably an overreaction, decided to play it cool. I grabbed the trash bag out of my oak gargoyle trashcan next to this desk, and headed downstairs as she jabbered, "He was next door talking to the Mexican guy that was working on the vacant house. He's just looking around casing the place. I need him to know a man lives here!"

The last thing I want is a confrontation, even if he is casing the place. I need to measure him, and he needs to know that I'm just normally out and about the house, not that I only appear when the wench cries 'negro!'

Of course, not only did she not lock the door, she had not even closed it. This chick doesn't last long in a horror movie.

I walked out onto the veranda and down the front walk to the trashcan as he was walking back past the plantation gate from the vacant next door. He had picked up a small envelope from on top of the trashcan and was opening it as he walked by me. I looked up to make respectful eye-contact, not hard-balling him, and he declined. He was a shy kid, about 16. A good looking lightweight I'd say.

It turns out that his mother lives two doors up in the large block rental where Peanut bags up his redcap and yellow cap and blue cap, and has the retarded kid sell it down by the gas station. She was going to be at work and wanted her estranged son to get his bus money—no info on why they are not cohabitating. Obviously she cannot trust her roommates. She did think she could trust the Mexican, so told him that she was leaving the envelope on one of the trashcans in front of the vacant for her son.

Interestingly enough the black lady next door was eying him suspiciously as well. This visual vigilance on the part of females is good. The problem is it has no teeth. In an urban environment on side streets it is good policy for the man to make himself visible, and visibly aware, while remaining respectful to passersby, not hostile or over friendly.

You do not want to seem to appear at the woman's call, or else, if this is someone casing the house, she becomes the first thing to get neutralized because she is the alarm system. You should just ask her nosey self to keep an eye out and then discretely let you know that someone is walking by—a male who appears fit enough to be a combatant—so that you can be noted as casually and unpredictably present and alert.

In this instance an automobile is a disadvantage. As soon as guys see me walk to and from the house they know that they will never be able to predict my presence unless they just saw me come or go. The vehicle pins you down. My roommate likes this about me, that even though he might be out on a business call that I might always be around. It seems like a small thing, but as with a large vigilant dog, just having a man visibly around takes the property way down to the bottom of the crime target list.

Most urban houses have no man. If you make yourself alertly and confidently visible on some of the occasions that young men are known to walk by, or when they appear suspiciously, you have done more to secure your property than getting an alarm system installed. Above all be cool and polite, not gregarious, not a rubbernecker, not insulting to the decent guys, which will be most who walk by, but just a man who seems with it enough to buy your dependents enough time to make that 911 call.

It is not enough to deter. You must not also insult, which could invite reprisals that are far worse than a simple property crime and more like what my female roommate, a suburban girl, feared. This kid had gang tattoos. There was nothing to be gained by showing him fear or disrespect, and much to be risked.

Awareness.

Presence.

Vigilance.

Poise.

Those four elements comprise most of the urban survival code that I have lived by since I came to Baltimore in 1981.

'What Are You Looking At?'

How to Answer this Perennial Jerk Challenge: A
Man Question from Alex in Athens

© 2014 James LaFond

Excellent question Alex. I did not know that jerks in
Athens Greece used the same lame line as jerks in
Baltimore Maryland when trying lamely to pick a
fight.

First of all, that is what we are talking about, a fight.
A fight is legally defined by our masters as a 'mutual
combat.' If the peace was not disturbed and
property was not destroyed, what this means is
that in court the winner is the loser and the loser is
the winner. Take note: if the law gets involved in
your 'fight' with this jerk, there is no winner.
Whoever does the most medical damage to the
other pays in court, and, if someone dies, the other
fool faces manslaughter charges.

Don't Get Boned

As a day dreaming writer, when in peaceful settings, I sometimes find that a person who I was inadvertently staring at becomes bothered by this, thinking it personal, when I might have been wondering about the dimensions of Soto's Noah, San Cristobal, and how many warhorses could be strapped on the second deck and how much horseshit this would produce, and how long each of the stable boys would have to shovel that shit overboard...

So, when asked this question by a passerby I have two stock answers, crafted to fit my urban setting and compliment the asker of the question based on gender alone.

The Bitch Challenge

If a black chick speaks up on the bus stop and says, "Excuse me Mister White, but what the hell you lookin' at?", what do I say in response?

"Oh, I'm sorry Miss. I was just trying to remember your name."

"Oh"—side-to-side head bobble—"you tryin' ta say I s'posed to know you?"

"Of course not, I was just one of the guys at the bar."

"What bar?"

"The El Dorado—you dance there on Saturday night, right?"

She then blushes, bats her eye-lids, and says in an embarrassed tone, "Oh I'm sorry Sir. I jus' thought you was, you know—You have a nice day Sir."

Not only do I get by that bit of embarrassment, she feels good about herself, and the young gangbanger next to me adopts me as an elder statesmen of the streets, and says to his partner, "Yo son, dat shit da hookup dare. Niggas knew how ta tame dey womenz back in his old-ass day, no doubt!"

The beauty of this tactic is, the less she looks like she belongs up on the stage at The El Dorado Lounge, the better it works!

The Jerk Challenge

When some young dumb buck full of animosity wants to pick a fight with me in this fashion and says, "What you lookin' at?", then what do I say?

"I was just trying to remember your name. It's been a while."

"What old man—I supposed ta know your or sometin'!"

"Oh, of course not, you've always got your eyes on your work when I see you. I'm one of the dudes that Vince lets sit ringside while you spar."

"Huh?"

"You fight out of the Eager Street Gym, right, Mister Mack's old place."

That is when his friends take over and begin laughing at him as his jaw drops in realization that he is being mistaken for a badass fighter that some super badass dude might want to whip, or that some punk like him will want to shoot. As his friends play-slap him and say, "Shit Old School thought you was somebody?", you could either make your exit with a respectful nod, or, if you are a boxing coach like me, walk up to him and give him a 'Combat Arts' card and say, "Really dude, you look like you got what it takes. Give me a call."

Conclusion

When it comes to this perennial and apparently global challenge, there is no better solution than diplomacy. Mind to keep on your guard though, that you are not being 'puffed up' for an attack by his friends. Even if that is the case it is still a reliable gambit.

And in case of the girl, if she is trying to set you up to get attacked by her boyfriend just include him as the bodyguard escorting her. You could swear he was the dude you saw shoving those drunks out of the way when she headed to the dressing room...

Running Wire

The Best Clue You Are in a Bad Neighborhood

© 2014 James LaFond

Oliver is a boxer who trains with our stick and knife-fighting club. He works in wiring, running cable for various cable TV concerns and as a subcontractor on construction sites, as well as supporting the efforts of computer installation contractors. We were in the locker room speaking with Parish, a young fellow who looks like he should be the guitarist for a black metal band, when Oliver [see Oliver on Stupid Shit and Taking out the Trash] put into perspective what weapons training has meant to him in everyday life.

"Earlier this year I was wiring behind this building in an alley of Greenmount Avenue—a real bad area. I'm on this sketchy ladder that looks like something that Lara Croft would be climbing in Tomb Raider. While I'm up on this thing I look down the alley and there are these dudes down there throwing dice, and they keep looking at me, talking about me. I just knew they were up to no good. Working in a bad area is worse than walking in a bad area. You have your back turned, your hands occupied.

"But now, thanks to this weapon perspective I have from doing this [agonistics] I look around at my environment and I see weapons everywhere. It's no longer just a space, but an arsenal. I look at these guys and climb down the ladder, go to my van, get my World War One bayonet—basically a can opening sword, and I use that to trim my wire.

"Now they're looking at me, and I'm looking at them trimming wire with this thing and then sticking it in the pole.

"They went back to spinning their dice."

"Anything is a weapon. Even those plastic knives and rolled up magazines we train with will knock a dude out. I've gotten to the point where I love knife fighting. The stick fighting is still scary until you get out there and get into it. But the knife is just such a real perspective on combat—there's no bullshit. As nasty as boxing is it has its bullshit. But the knife, that cuts through all that."

So, what is the best clue that you are in a bad neighborhood?

That's right, dudes throwing dice in the alley, the more of them there are the worse the area is. Find a brick or a pipe—if a WWI bayonet is not handy— and get your ass to the busiest street and drop your weapon in the gutter before the cops jack you up for threatening the criminal class they are sworn to protect and house.

At The Bar

A Logic of Force Addendum on the Classic Drunken Jerk

© 2014 James LaFond

Bradley was at a roadhouse bar outside of Hanover, PA, a favorite haunt from years gone by, with a men's room built over an old converted screened in porch. Brad just stopped in for a couple of beers. He's a big man nearing retirement; a long haul trucker originally from Texas. Brad is one of the more mild mannered people I have interviewed, a real gentleman in a manchild world.

He had noticed Susanne when he came in and had said hello. She is a longtime friend of his youngest son. She seemed to be there with friends and having a good time so he didn't stop to talk.

After a beer or so Susanne came up to the bar and said, "Mister Brad is it okay if I stand here next to you. This guy has been bothering me and I don't want to have to talk to him."

Brad just nodded 'yes' to her and cast an eye on the fellow she was speaking of. The offensive drunk was a young thin man who seemed of little account.

After a few minutes the creep squeezed up to the bar between Susanne and Brad and elbowed him, not a strike, but a needling grind in his side.

Brad said, "Do you mind?"

The man stopped, and then. Moments later, did it again.

Brad warned him not to do it again.

The man did it again.

Brad said to the bartender, "Hey Harvey, please tell this guy to stop touching me."

Harvey translated the request into barkeep speak. Even after the bartender spoke to him the creep continued with the elbow. Brad seized him by the seat of the pants and the collar, lifted him into the air, and smashed his upper half into the bar top.

The fellow had been surprisingly light, even for a scrawny guy. Harvey told Brad to leave and he did. The revived fool was then made to leave after Brad had cleared out.

This event is represented in my original 1,675 account survey from the late 1990s by about 300 lines of checked off boxes. This type of thing has become all but none existent in Baltimore City. When I do get such accounts it comes courtesy of bikers and truckers like Dante and Brad. Most bar fights are not worthy of the name and fall into this category of one-sided dominant acts that barely rise to the level of an 'altercation'. In urban environments 'fools' like the 'elbow guy' generally supply strong arm mugging victims, targets for thrill stompings and gang jump-ins, as well as easy arrests for loitering, public intoxication, and possession.

The Complete Pimp Slap

A Graduate Course with Ray Ray Ravens Rice!

© 2014 James LaFond

Class, this section is not about the theory and philosophy of pimping, but is rather a comprehensive examination of the Pimp's most reliable and off misunderstood tools. Before we continue please break off and view—if you have not already—former ravens running back Ray Rice in his altercation with his darling wife in an Atlantic City elevator. It is available at TMZ. I have viewed this video the sacred seven times and will begin with the version of the pimp slap used by Ray Ray, and go onto variants and applications.

The Pimp Hand

The pimp hand is used in five applications which are adversary specific. Ray Ray, being a stupid football player who requires a coach to tell him what to do, selected the wrong application for the adversary at hand and is in the process of paying the resulting price. So, my aspiring pimp, just in case you should find yourself on video and being attacked by a female and you do not have myself of Jim Brown standing behind you intoning sage advice in your ear, here go da arsenal yo:

1. The bitch slap

2. The taste removal slap

3. The monsta bitch slap

4. The ho slap

5. And the pimp slap proper

The Bitch Slap

The technique Ray Ray used is identical to a shovel hook, only with an open hand. He did not punch her, but threw a diagonal rising hook from the hip. This is a blow that is—in boxing—favored by narrow assed Mexicans and on the street by narrow-assed pimps like Huggy Bear from Starsky and Hutch. Ray has a little too much ass to put behind this where a shorty or petite is concerned.

The bitch slap is used to stop a man of less than formidable physicality or a big bitch like Pam Grier or Venus Williams. Against this little lady it was overkill on Ray's part. Ray Ray popped her like he was Tiger Woods and she was some pissed off Viking chick with a 9-iron.

Of course Ray's wench did run into this full tilt and ate a lot of force. If you are hitting someone with an open hand and they are charging and you have no intention of incapacitating them, turn it into a push. This woman's head was farther forward then her shoulders and had all of her weight forward.

Also, keep in mind that if Ray Ray had been wearing a Chinchilla fur coat, a ruffled fur scarf, and a pimp hat the camera would have not been able to track his hand from behind and would have only shown the reverse crane's beak chambered above the right shoulder, which could be explained away of you had not knocked her out Ray!

The Taste Removal Slap

Notice as you freeze the video right as the little lady's head is about to meet the railing, that Ray's left hand is open and above his right shoulder.

From this position, you say over your bicep, in an even tone, and if she is not running her mouth, in a whisper, "Girl, chill fo I slap da taste right out yo mouth!"

This line, if delivered evenly, and behind a judiciously placed bitch slap, should obviate the need for the delivery of the back hand, laterally across the lips. Note that if you are looking forward to makeup sex this should be avoided as her lips will be all busted up. Also, do not attempt this with a monsta bitch.

The Monsta Bitch Slap

For really big women like Queen Latifah and Serena Williams, or against formidable men, you want to hit them as hard as possible by pivoting with the left leg and rolling your shoulder through. Maximum power will be achieved at the point where your forearm is parallel with the jaw, the jaw being the target.

Additionally if a monsta bitch is charging, you must deploy the rear hand to check her forward progress as you pivot out to the left. You do not want her getting a hold of your junk before she goes into her alligator death roll.

The Ho Slap

A discerning pimp reserves this weapon for use against nappy headed hood rat hos who threaten his girls or otherwise impinge on the ghetto peace.

The technique is the same as demonstrated by Ray, only you grab the hard headed ho by her fro and hold her up for a talking to.

This may seem cruel. But please—you liberal white people—keep in mind that the hardest heads in America are to be found in boxing gyms and ghetto hair salons. If Ray Ray's girl would have been completely white she might have died from the triple head impact with NFL palm, steel rail, and steel floor.

The Pimp Slap Proper

You grab your girl with either hand by the hair. If she's as good looking as Ray Ray's babe that is a $1000 head of hair; either tracks that could pull her real hair out by the roots, or real hair that is so brittle from chemical treatments that it could be broken.

The actual slap is from the elbow and just enough to get her attention, a conversation starter. If she is really your girl you need this to be a pat, a 'Hey Baby, I'm your protector. Let's talk this out.'

The Next Course Section

Class, the next time we meet, we will delve into pimp theory and philosophy, and the contention that the remnant pimps among us are the last best hope for civilization.

Delivering Funeral Flowers

Two Innocent Unarmed Black Teens in Action

© 2014 James LaFond

Bryce works for a Northeast Baltimore florist and was delivering flowers to an East Baltimore funeral home. After he left his car and began walking the delivery down the sidewalk two innocent unarmed black teens approached him from behind, and said the following:

IUBT #1: "Yo, what you gonna do 'bout dat Yo?"

IUBT #2: "Oh I jack a muvafuca fo anyting."

IUBT #1: "Yo, yo jackin; dis muvafuca fo 'is shit?"

IUBT #2: "Shee Yo, I 'bout ta jack dis bitch right hea!"

Bryce was carrying a large wrought iron-style steel-tube basket of flowers in his left hand at hip level, and had a thick glass vase of flowers couched in his right arm. As he heard the trash-talking cease and the footfalls come closer he turned, setting the basket down at his feet and cocking back the water-filled glass vase as a missile.

"They stopped right in their tracks and we locked eyes. I suppose the brave one with the mouth did the physics and decided that his skull was about to fail upon collision with the hard object in my hand. They just backed off, and they were a few steps away when the smaller guy—they were both in their mid-teens—said, "Yo, I thought you would jack anybody fo dey shit?"

Sadly enough this stillborn stupid moment demonstrates the extent of the motivation, planning and resolve of most black youth on white adult crimes, which are generally not displays of dominance behavior or predation, but bonding activities.

Boys, who have been abused by their mothers, neglected by their fathers since infancy, and told by one and all that they are 'little men' from diapers to cargo shorts are busily trying to invent a manhood matrix that will provide a ladder out of their pit of denatured despair. Here in Harm City attacking some large pale herd animal as a pack member seems to be the preferred rite of passage into thughood.

Surviving A Punchout

Keeping Your Teeth in Your Head

© 2014 James LaFond

Last Friday night I got to work to find that Mushmouth Mike had been threatening to punch out Big Bubba, specifically threatening to knockout his young teeth, which I suppose is a point of jealousy common to 65 point IQ owners of false teeth. As Bubba checked out my drink before I began toiling for The Man, Steevo said, "Hey Jim, Mike wants to beat up Bubba. Don't you think you ought to give him a lesson so he can defend himself?"

I just smiled and nodded knowing Bubba to be one of those guys who is so nice it would pretty much be a waste of time to teach him how to fight, and I train fighters. I do not teach self-defense.

Mike was avoiding Steevo, who is cinder-block head last choice on the crew for guy you want to fight in an alley. Since I'm the odd man out he sucked up to me. This behavior from someone who has just threatened bodily harm struck me as craven. If we were a band of mountain men I would have scalped him right then and there. So, upon consideration, and knowing that Bubba reads this blog, I have decided to give him what advice is appropriate from a boxing coach concerning surviving a punchout.

#1 Beware the sucker punch. Most sucker punches are effective and target taller men, as the key is access to the chin and jaw, which is the lever that short circuits the transmission of messages from the brain to the body.

#2 Know the punch is coming if possible by keeping an eye on the dirt bag.

#3 Tuck your chin and shrug your shoulders to minimize access to your jaw and shock to your neck.

#4 Step back with one foot as you tuck and shrug so that you have a brake that will keep you from falling and bashing your head on something harder than that asshole's fist. You are about to get hit, but if he does not clip the chin and is not some kind of beast or trained fighter you will ride it out.

Don't Get Boned

#5 Do not punch back and do not get hit again. Hang your arms over his arms then pull them in and hook your arms up under his from behind. Place your head next to his head over the shoulder so that he cannot head butt, bite off your nose, or spit or blow snot on you. Warning: If he is a vampire and/or prone to bite, or would be played by an Italian actor if this were the basis for a mafia movie, place your skull under his chin so he can't rip out your neck or take off your ear.

#6 He will try to pull his arms free. Work this 'over hook' clinch tight as you step on his feet. He will eventually get one arm lose. When this happens step close to the other side and hook the other arm high and tight, trying to rip it up and off his body [Don't worry, it won't actually come off unless you are a cyborg.] as you place the palm of your other hand on his far shoulder and continue to tuck your chin. If he keeps at it trip him and fall on top of him with your legs spread as you pull up with your arm. This will separate his shoulder and reduce his combat ability to almost nothing and also seriously compromise his video gaming score.

#7 Just hold onto this jerk like you life depends on it. Let a third party break it up.

Don't Get Boned

That is the best advice I have for someone who is not a boxer or grappler for defending against a punch out attempt by an individual who is known to them. What I have described is the most used defense against punching in the boxing ring, and requires no skill.

'Yo Yo, yo!'

Can You Translate That Sentence? An Ebonic Grammatical Timeout

© 2014 James LaFond

I have gotten lucky and landed a editor for my multi-million word Sunset Saga series of novels, which is saving me 160 hours. The lady is working from her home in rural America, in God's Country as my grandmother used to say.

She sent me an email an hour ago suggesting that I have worn the 'yo' joke kind of thin:

"Are you referencing the old cartoon 'Billy and Mandy' with the amount of times Eddie says "yo"?

No Dear, Eddie's 'yo' usage is at the median frequency of black urban youth.

[Eddie, by the way, is a reformed East Baltimore crack dealer who has managed to attach himself to a time-travel organization as a gofer and ends up in over his head often.]

Don't Get Boned

Below is a sentence which I shall translate for you on the following line:

"Yo Yo, yo!

"Hey my-special-friend, lookout!"

As you can see the brevity of the diction makes for more efficient communication during such hairy situations as drug deals and busts. Also, the severely limited vocabulary is easily mastered before the age of 8 when boys are first recruited as runners and lookouts. This is just one of many reasons that police departments, saddled as they are with the archaic English language, are so hopelessly overmatched on the street.

Now let's flex our ebonic muscles a little more, with a sentence that might be employed by a high level operator.

"Yo Yo, Yo's shit be fucked-up, Yo."

"Hey my-special-friend that dude's money is wrong and I think he is stealing, just-between-you-and-me."

Let me break it down vertically:

Don't Get Boned

"Yo [Hey]

Yo [my-special-friend]

Yo's [that dude's]

shit [money]

be [is]

fucked-up, [wrong-and I think he is stealing]

Yo." [just-between-you-and-me]

So now, T-Bob and Blood-Bone have, by reducing 20 words to 8, gained the three crucial seconds necessary to bum rush their partner in crime before he even gets his hands out of his pockets.

Try pulling that off in English!

Home Is Where The Harm Is

A Breakdown of the 50 Most Recent Harm City Attacks on Men

© 2014 James LaFond

Who Is Being Attacked?

0 elderly or disabled black men

5 black men

5 black youths

7 elderly or disabled white men

29 white men

3 white youths

Who Are the Aggressors?

4 lone white criminals

3 mixed-race criminal groups

4 black women [domestic attacks on male partners]

5 pairs of white police officers

1 mixed race pair of police officers

1 lone black police officer

5 lone black criminals

27 groups of black criminals

Notes

1. The only whites involved in attacks on blacks are police officers.

2. Of the 4 lone white criminals 1 was unarmed, 1 was gun-armed, 1 knife-armed, and 1 was armed with a mallet

3. Of the 5 lone black criminals 1 was unarmed, 2 were knife-armed, and 2 were gun-armed

4. Of the 4 black women 1 was knife-armed, 1 club-armed, and 2 unarmed

5. Of the 5 black men attacked 4 were attacked by black women and 1 by a pair of black youths

6. Of the 30 criminal groups only one was armed, with a single member having a knife, this indicates that group tactics have superseded armed tactics as a means of avoiding criminal charges.

7. Of the 43 violent crimes only 4 were reported to the police, a fatal shooting, a fatal stabbing, a vigilante beating, and the stabbing of a woman by three youths. No arrests were made in connection with the beating or non-fatal stabbing.

8. Of the 7 police aggressions 5 targeted black youths and 2 white adults

Conclusion

I am no longer collecting accounts full time, with these 50 incidents being incidentally recorded over the past 3 years. This is not a broad enough sample to predict risks beyond the North/Northeast Baltimore to Eastern Baltimore County axis which I frequent.

The 2 dominant numbers reflect the fact that most violent crimes in Northeast Baltimore involve groups of black men and youth attacking lone white adult males. The lone aggressors demonstrate similar behaviors across racial lines.

Stopping the Twerp Knife Rampage

Unarmed Measures against Small Marginal Knifers

© 2014 James LaFond

This past weekend I saw news about a knife rampage by a boy near Pittsburgh who stabbed many people before he was stopped, and, based on his appearance, fit the twerp mold to a T. To be clear, a 'twerp' is someone who has picked up a knife because they can't take care of business with their empty hands. The twerp is a creature that you could definitely squash in an empty hand encounter.

I prefer improvised weapons versus the twerp if alone. If you are alone treat the twerp like a goon and take no chances. However, if you are coming to the aid of others less able than yourself—and particularly if they are cute and single—your safety comes second. You must not think like a cop here, but like a warrior.

First you must be able to clearly make the twerp or goon call. It is not all about size. Uriah Faber with a bowie knife does not type as a twerp. Once you have determined that this twerp is a twerp you need to run his ass over.

That's right. Imagine you are a dump truck and he is a Smartcar, or better yet, that he is Tom Brady and you are 350 pounds of angry African American defensive back.

This advise is based on thousands of hours of full contact knife sparring with wooden blunts and hundreds of duels with steel blunts. Despite all the FMA bullshit there are only two answers when you lose your knife in a duel: run your ass off, or run his ass over. In a knife duel you have a split second in which you know your weapon is leaving your hand and he does not. That is when you crash the range barrier. During a rampage the knifer is moving from target to target as fast as possible and is conditioned to flight, submission and struggle on the point of his victims. Running at him is not expected.

1. Place your left palm under the left line of your jaw, with your thumb and forefinger extending toward the ear.

2. Tuck your chin.

3. Extend your right hand in a pronated [palm down] half-fist.

4. Hit him as fast as you can to cause sensory shock and get him off his feet.

5. Go to the floor with him and hold him with your legs and your teeth while you use your hands to control his knife hand and separate it from the other hand by getting his body and head between them.

6. If the knife has been ejected and he is scrambling for it I like to get both hands on his head at the base and do a push up, touching the floor with my toes only as all of my weight pins his neck and head against the floor.

If this guy is your size or larger, or if he seems to be particularly athletic or vicious with the knife, treat him as a goon.

Stopping the Goon Knife Rampage

Desperate Measures against the Rampaging Knifer Who Could Take You without the Knife

© 2014 James LaFond

This past weekend I saw a news report about some wannabe Islamist in Oklahoma who cut a female coworker's head off and stabbed another before the CEO stopped him with gunfire. The leftist press gave the CEO a pass for oppressing this starving brother because he was some kind of part time cop. Also, the reporters knew instinctively after seeing this goon's mug shot that they would have been prison yard sushi in seconds.

Last night two coworkers and a friend asked me what could be done against such an attacker in the absence of a firearm, which usually is absent and will one day be banned altogether.

The goon is the knifer that could kick your ass without the knife. This is an OJ Simpson Situation

I'm talking about. The thing that freaks cops about goons is that cops are trained to get close and take you down and the goon wants to get close and take you apart with a weapon more appropriate for that range than anything on the cop's utility belt. By the looks of the mug shot this fellow was a 20-something African American of good size. Nobody in that front office was going to be able to outrun this buck.

In such a situation the women, the elderly, the children and the hesitant are dead meat. If you are a real man and would rather risk life and limb than see the kind of butchery that is going to commence on a regular basis in American public spaces and work places as soon as firearms are removed from U.S. society, you need to be able to fight with extension weapons.

The best weapons against a knife are, in order of preference, but unfortunately in a generally reverse order of availability:

1. Crow bar

2. Axe handle

3. Steel door pipe [found on exterior doors in supermarkets and other retail stockrooms]

4. **Dairy hook [a long soft iron bar with a handle and a dull hook used to drag stacks of milk crates—hit a hole in one with his head!]

5. Fireplace poker

6. **Steel shovel [chop-thrust into his face and throat from a high guard, then chop his hands off when he goes down]

7. Fire extinguisher

8. *Barstool

9. *Folding metal chair

10. Fixed wood or pipe frame chair

11. Commercial trashcan

12. Pool cue snapped off to a 3 foot length

13. A pitcher of beer or any bottle

14. Gallons of anything, bleach being the best, heaved with both hands at his chest

15. Canned goods used as missile weapons. Extend your left had as you cock for the throw as it will help your aim.

16. Bat

17. **Two-by-four

18. **Electric guitar

19. A small to medium-sized dog held by the hind legs [once used by a friend against a knifer] or a cat held by the tale and whipped in one hand

20. Hammer [turn him into hamburger]

21. Screwdriver [slam it into his face—it will go in]

22. A block or brick [knife rampages on construction sites should be short-lived]

23. ***The upright end frame handle of a retail U-boat [you need to be stronger than average] which are set loose in sockets on either end of the rolling platform

24. Commercial Mop bucket or the strainer, which should be swung two handed by the handle and used to de-flesh the face

25. **Toilet seat [It will come right off. Hold it by both the open ends and swing it like the capital C from hell]

26. Rolling chair

27. Five-gallon pail

28. Appliance such as TV, monitor, microwave

29. Shopping cart [run at him with it, smash his shins, and then dump the basket over his head and jump up and down on any feet or hands that stick out]

30. Wooden shelving or aluminum shelf molding [the tag stripping on dairy and frozen food cases makes a dull whippy sword

31. Anything longer and harder than the knife

*The most practical of the easily accessible weapons are stools and chairs. Stools can be gripped by the seat to fend off [knock his teeth down his throat] and pin a knifer or reversed as a pole axe. A folding chair should be closed and used to fend and pin with a grip on the bar and the seat back, and also makes a great pole-axe when held by the legs.

**Heavy extension weapons should be used at range as a pole axe. Practice making a rising 'i' loop and a falling reverse 'Q' loop. A pole-axe without a blade should not be used to chop but rather in sweeping motions that facilitate a flowing return stroke. If you gave me a folding metal chair or bar stool and gave any NFL player a butcher knife and tossed us into a pit, I would murder him. People have no idea how nasty extension weapons can be until they have fought with them, as martial arts defense sets and movie stunts always characterize the use of such weapons in the most ineffective ways possible.

Just remember, if you brought a troop of medieval warriors out of the past and let them select their weapons at the Home Depot, knives would be the last things they'd picked up.

Coyote Elbow—Ghetto Style

Notes on Living Next to a Vacant

© 2014 James LaFond

It is 4:45 a.m. Sunday, October 12, 2014. 15 minutes ago I was awakened by the slamming of the door downstairs by the female roommate who had been on the porch smoking and was approached by a man on foot who came from a car parked in the driveway next door. By the time she was upstairs sounding the alarm one of the other men in the house was on the porch.

I joined him to see that the new model metallic 4-door was still parked in the drive in front of the scrap dumpster. He checked the ground floor windows from the interior while I stayed on the porch. He returned to the porch while I checked the basement—me being the runt I feel honor bound to act as house tunnel rat.

Don't Get Boned

When I returned upstairs he informed me that the car was moving out with two individuals in it. It was now halted on the street in front of the vacant. We walked down to get a license plate number, which he could not read without his glasses and I could not remember, but which the both of us together could record.

The large driver was getting nervous so the smaller passenger opened the door [thus illuminating the interior for us] to claim, "Sorry, he was going to the wrong house. I live in the next house up [a house where a drug dealer lives but where she does not]. Sorry, he's just dropping me off."

They then pulled up to the rental two doors down and idled. He was a large light skinned black man about 30 and she a small white woman about 40 who sounded seventy. Once we returned inside my female roommate asked if she should call the police and I said, "No. You do not want to be fingering a drug operation two doors down when they know the call came from you. This guy probably picked up this girl at a black bar—they stay open until four; just stop serving drinks at two and people load up and make arrangements to take things to the next level elsewhere. This was probably sex for drugs behind the dumpster. The guy was nervous and pissed at her—he thinks he's scoring a white woman before going home to his wife. He's not a dealer. The dealer in the house is also pissed at her because he does not retail from the house and she is bringing potential heat. Let them be mad at her, not you."

In such situations I do not recommend showing aggression outside of your property borders. We did go slightly beyond to get the license number but only due to poor eye-sight. Also, there is nothing an ordinary police officer can do about the dealer in the house other than to let him know that you are a threat. The best policy for an urban household is to threaten only two things: defense of the home, and retaliation by or vengeance for members caught alone on the street.

Do not become a threat to their home or business unless your people are attacked, because their reinforcements will be proactive and represent their interests, where the police will be reactive and represent the municipal interests, which do not include protecting individual residences or the 'right' of the residents to walk freely down the street, but those of commercial businesses. If you own a business and this happens the police will usually act in your interest.

Don't Get Boned

The household female has decided to arrange for lighting on the side of the house which is the best antidote to the use of the space between our home and the vacant as a 'tweener space' by addicts, hookers, criminals, the homeless, werewolves, and vampires, but not stoner zombies such as the ones I ran into the night before last.

The Harm City Shuffle

Two Innocent, Unarmed Black Teens Attack Black Man on Subway in Baltimore and the Brits Think it's News

© 2014 James LaFond

Brooklyn Shane sent me this link and demanded—said it was mandatory—that I do an article on it, or I suppose some dude named Vinnie shows up at my door....

Yes Sir!

Okay, according to the MTA this was probably at the Mondawmin station, which is right next to where Miss Ezz works at Cheap Guys R' Us, often featured in my Ghetto Grocer articles.

First to the important aspect of this incident: it was filmed by Diana Benbow, an ebony babe who I have viewed a few times from the comfort of my seat aboard the #22 and #8. She has a long waist, smells very nice, and apparently squeezes her petite self into her jeans while they are wet. Good work Diana. If you need a safe house while the heat is blowing over after your fine bit of video journalism the room above mine is for rent—but free to you I think. What can I say, I've got connections Boo.

Now onto the ancillary matters.

People were actually surprised that no one stepped up to help. Look, these are black kids, they either belong to a gang, in which case their older set members will avenge them, or they are innocent unarmed teens whose mother probably works for the city government and will sue your ass off. I have watched dozens of gang attacks on individuals and have never leant a hand.

Are you people stupid, or just British?

Once when getting off the #44 bus I thought I was being attacked by three kids, but before I could slash the big kid's nuts off with my razor he was beating a kid that had been standing next t me. So I said to myself, "Wew, not me," folded the razor back up, and went about my business.

Don't Get Boned

Look, if someone grabbed one of these kids they would be committing a violent crime against a minor. A cop who grabbed one of these kids would go under review!

These Brits—obviously progressive socialists—profess to be in shock that this man, who did successfully defend himself, did not call the police. Okay, the guy looks to be about my age—in his fifties maybe. I get hassled by cops—got threatened by one last night in fact, while I was working in a grocery store—at least 1 time per year, and I'm a member of the Master Race. A black man in Baltimore who is not a preacher or a government worker will be beaten or arrested randomly by cops on average once per decade. That means this guy has probably had cops do this to him 4 times—and much more effectively—where these punks have probably only been beaten once each by cops. He has more reason to hate the cops than they.

Please.

Also, the subway in Baltimore is very limited, and basically goes nowhere. Most of this stuff happens at bus stops. My best guess is the motivation for this attack was that the man previously defended himself against one of these punks and a third party who was somewhere out in the ghetto watching the blood drip from his nose onto the pavement. Revenge for a successful defense is the most common reason for such a public attack in Harm City.

10/16/14, Update: A friend just informed me that this altercation was based on the youths objecting to the man holding the door for another passenger.

The bright light here is the video posted on social media by a citizen. This will eventually be outlawed, and people like my future roommate who take the publishing of potential evidence into their own delicate hands, will be arrested and charged. But for now, we can enjoy technology permitting us to bipass the media filers, for this would never get on TV first, or make the paper in Baltimore, if a citizen had not put it out there first.

http://www.dailymail.co.uk/news/article-2793991/terrifying-video-shows-two-teenagers-rip-open-doors-moving-train-try-throw-elderly-man-nearby-witnesses-stop-them.html

Thank you for reading this Harm City Book, and please, Don't Get Boned!